# LifeSong

## *My Symphony*

BY
KAREN TWIGG

LifeSong - My Symphony

Copyright ©2013 Karen Twigg
Printed in the United States of America
ISBN 978-0-9894026-3-7

All rights reserved solely by the author. The author guarantees all contents are original and do not infringe upon the legal rights of any other person or work. No part of this book may be reproduced in any form without the permission of the author.

The views expressed in this book are not necessarily those of the publisher.

All references unless otherwise noted are from
All Bible references are from the Holy Bible authorized
King James Version – New Schofield Reference Bible   1967

Luke 15:25 • John 3:16 • Isaiah 6:8 • 1 Thessalonians 5:24
Joshua 1:9 • Psalm 100 • 23 Psalm

Contact Karen at:
Email:
LifeSong_MySymphony@yahoo.com

Address:
LifeSong or Karen Twigg or Leslie Geisendaffer
PO Box 160531, Altamonte Springs, FL 32716-0531

www.trueperspectivepublishinghouse.com

# Endorsements

*As a parent and a minister of the gospel, I see Karen Twigg as a woman of faith. Karen has opened her life as a book for all to see and quite possible learn from the error of her ways. But this story was not about Karen, it is about God getting the glory for the good things He has done in her life. Karen Twigg has always served the Lord. And it is evident from her trials and tribulations that the Lord was in her midst at all times. Never was she truly alone for the Lord was always at her side. This is a book for young women the world over to read and learn. This book teaches them that If God be for you, then no one can be against you. The Lord protected and delivered Karen Twigg through all her trials and tribulation and He certainly can deliver you. Please buy a copy of this book and give it to your daughters and the young women of your church. God is love and He has certainly demonstrated this in the life of Karen Twigg.*

**C.G. Walwyn, Commissioner of Police - Associate Pastor**
**Commissioner of Police Saint Kitts and Nevis**
**Royal Saint Christopher and Nevis Police Force**
**Great Mount Carmel Missionary Baptist Church**
**Tangerine, Orange County, Florida**

*"Karen Twigg's life is a true symphony of God's grace and faithfulness. I'm proud to be a small part of the big things He is doing in her lifesong."*
**Pastor Clint Brown**
**Faithworld Church, Orlando Fl.**

*I was given a copy of Karen Twigg's book to read by a local pastor. As a mother of three daughters, I believe that the strength that Karen Twigg displayed while going through her storm, needs to be seen by every young woman in high school and college and every single mother going through turmoil. Karen is truly a testimony for single mothers everywhere who can look at Karen as proof that their strength cometh from the Lord. Karen Twigg is truly an inspiration and the book is a must read for young women everywhere. To God be the glory for the great things he has done in Karen Twigg's life and the women who will read her book.*
**Orlando, Florida**
**Antoinette "Toni" Walwyn**
"Why is it that our children can't read a Bible in school, but they can read one in jail?"

*Every life is a story waiting to be told and no two are ever the same. Karen's life is no exception. In her "Symphony ", all the experiences, challenges and opportunities in her life, come together to create her personal masterpiece. As in music, some of life's notes are high, some low, some sharp, some flat. Add in powerful crescendos of opportunity and barely audible tones of despair; toss in a cappella verses without instrumental accompaniment where the voice stands alone. They are all part of her life, her song. It's said, "It isn't what happens to us that matters, but rather what we do with what happens to us that makes a difference." Karen's life is a testimony to her unwavering faithfulness and trust in God. She knows now, as she has always known...........
He will provide, He will comfort and sustain. He will see her through. As you read about her amazing life experiences and her triumphs over adversity, I hope you enjoy the concert as I have!*
**Caryl Brigance – Security Area Manager at Walt Disney World** (one of Karen's bosses)

# Dedication

*To Every Reader*

This book is dedicated to every reader that God brings to these pages. He told me to write it for you. Read it seeking which part(s) are just for you. Don't doubt it is for you because you have it in your hands now as God ordained it as part of the Symphony. Open your mind to receive God's messages and lessons portrayed through my LifeSong. *I am praying for you!*

# Acknowledgements

*Leslie, my precious child*

You have stood by me through the majority of LifeSong. You have encouraged me, understood me, and been patient with me every step of the way through the 15 years preparing this book. You are the most special daughter, the greatest blessing I have ever had. Now that we are publishing the book we are beginning a brand new movement in our life's symphony. Thank you for coming with me on the journey. You are beautiful inside and out, so caring for everyone, especially your Mom. *I love you!*

*Amanda, my special grand daughter*

WOW you have had to hear about this book and music for the majority of your life. You have encouraged me along the way. As you were growing up I was living/writing LifeSong. Your words after proof reading the book were "You have done so much to help people". I see that in you as you are always reaching out to others. You are so precious to me. My very first financial gift for LifeSong was a check you earned for a job you did. Your support, words and suggestions have been very beneficial to the completion of this project. We have so many more verses to share in our LifeSong. *I love you!*

*To all who put up with me through the years, continuously talking about the book and CD*

There are so many of you who encouraged and assisted in parts of this project: praying for me, listening to me share the stories and music, transcribing the tapes, proofreading and correcting, listening to the CD. I never heard anyone say they were tired of hearing about it (although I was a bit obsessive at times). Don't stop praying for me now. I pray for you and ask God to bless you for your part in *LifeSong - My Symphony*.

*Special thanks to Melinda and Cody*

Thank you, Melinda Davis, for being such a great friend to my Leslie. Your front cover design says it all. And Cody Thomas, thanks for making me look so good. Great picture!

LIFESONG - MY SYMPHONY

# Autograph Page

*Autograph this book to yourself or a friend who is still working on their life's symphony*

*Joshua 1:9*
*Have not I commanded thee? Be strong and of good courage; be not afraid, neither be thou dismayed; for the Lord your God is with thee wherever thou goest.*

# Life is a Symphony

Life is a symphony
Since the man from Galilee
Changed my discord in to song
Made life sweet
The whole day long
Life is a symphony
Since the man from Galilee
No more a stranger
He is the arranger
Of my symphony

*- Beatrice Bush Baxter*

## *My Interlude -*

Life is a Symphony
My LifeSong sings for Thee
Through all eternity
I'll praise your name

*Karen -2008*

# *LifeSong – My Symphony*

*From Wikipedia, the free encyclopedia*

## Symphony - "Sounding Together"

The word *symphony* is derived from the Greek Συμφωνία, a combination of *syn-* ('συν', with, together) and *phone* ('φωνή', sound, sounding), by way of the Latin *symphonia*.

In the Gospel of Luke, chapter 15 verse 25, it is distinguished from χορῶν, and the passage is appropriately translated in the English Bible as "music and dancing".

### Luke 15:25
### *Now his elder son was in the field; and as he came and drew near to the house, he heard music and dancing.*

The main characteristics of the symphony, as it existed by the end of the 18th century in the German-speaking world were: *4 movements*, of which the first would usually be a fast movement in sonata form, the second a slow movement, the third either a minuet and trio or a ternary dance-like *(scherzo)* movement in "simple triple" metre, finishing with a fourth, fast movement in rondo and/or sonata form.

*The normal four movement form became, then:*

1. **Quick, in a binary form or later sonata form**
2. **Slow**
3. **Minuet and trio (later developed into the scherzo and trio), in ternary form**
4. **Quick, sometimes also in sonata form. Other common possibilities are Rondo form or sonata-rondo**

# *Song -*

*"Art songs are songs created for performance in their own right, or for the purposes of a European upper class, usually with piano accompaniment." Generally they have an identified author(s) and require voice training for acceptable performances.*

A song is a relatively short musical composition. It is typically for a solo singer, though may also be a duet, trio, or more voices. Songs are typically of a poetic, rhyming nature, although they may be religious verses or free prose. Songs can be broadly divided into many different forms, depending on the criteria used. One division is between "art songs", "popular music songs", and "folk songs". Other common methods of classification are by purpose (sacred vs secular), by style (dance, ballad, Lieder, etc.) or by time of origin (Renaissance, Contemporary, etc).

Colloquially, *song* is often used to refer to any music composition, even those without vocals.

**A structural analysis of a typical pop song is in this order:**
**1. Introduction**
**2. Verse**
**3. Chorus**
**4. Verse**
**5. Chorus**
**6. Instrumental Bridge**
**7. Repeat chorus to fade**

*I relate my life to a song, created for a specific purpose, a life that has been accompanied by my piano, authored by God. My entire life has been a training ground preparing me for each movement in* **LifeSong - My Symphony.**

*Karen*

# TABLE OF CONTENTS

## INTRODUCTION

### CHAPTER 1:  IN REGARDS TO WORK         -- MEDLEY--

- No Job ................................................................................................ Page 15
- First Job - Telephone Company ....................................................... Page 18
- Jamaica ............................................................................................. Page 18
- Church Secretary ............................................................................. Page 19
- Telephone Company – My Mission Field ........................................ Page 19
- Teaching ........................................................................................... Page 21

### CHAPTER 2:  CHILDHOOD    -- SONATA/Quick--Verse/Solo --

- Family ............................................................................................... Page 23
- Camp Sequanota .............................................................................. Page 25
- Church - Music ................................................................................. Page 26
- Meyersdale ....................................................................................... Page 28

### CHAPTER 3:  MY YOUTH         --Slow--Verse/Chorus

- Ohio – I Accepted The Free Gift Of Salvation ................................. Page 33
- High School Days ............................................................................. Page 35
- Music, Music, Music ......................................................................... Page 37
- Relationships .................................................................................... Page 40
- Almost Suicide – Attack ................................................................... Page 43

### CHAPTER 4:  JAMAICA         --MINUET--Interlude

- The Call – Precious Lord Take My Hand ......................................... Page 47
- The Mission Field ............................................................................. Page 50
- Teach - Learn - Preach ..................................................................... Page 51
- Piano ................................................................................................. Page 54
- Missionary Friends .......................................................................... Page 55
- Yield To Temptation ......................................................................... Page 56

# LIFESONG - MY SYMPHONY

# TABLE OF CONTENTS

### CHAPTER 5: OHIO – THE RETURN      --TRIO-- Bridge
- *Admitting Failure – Getting Up and Going Again* ...................... *Page 63*
- *Offerings* ................................................................................. *Page 64*
- *He Touched Me – While Serving* ............................................. *Page 65*
- *The Call – Baptist Bible College* .............................................. *Page 67*

### CHAPTER 6: MISSOURI      --SCHERZO—Verse/Duet
- *Getting Settled* ........................................................................ *Page 69*
- *My Tribute* .............................................................................. *Page 71*
- *The Deaf* .................................................................................. *Page 77*
- *Raising Leslie*
    - *Signing Together* ............................................................... *Page 78*
    - *Dance & Pageants* .............................................................. *Page 78*
    - *Mother & Daughter* ............................................................ *Page 79*
- *Work - Promotion* .................................................................. *Page 80*
- *Teaching & The Deaf* ............................................................... *Page 82*
- *Relationships* .......................................................................... *Page 85*
- *Holidays* .................................................................................. *Page 89*
- *More Life - Loss - Green Peppers* ............................................ *Page 91*

### CHAPTER 7: FLORIDA -- RONDO/Quick-Verse/Duet & Chorus
*Project Rock* ............................................................................. *Page 100*
*Family Ties* ............................................................................... *Page 100*
*Another Job Ends - Leslie Leaves* ............................................. *Page 101*
*Darden Restaurants* ................................................................. *Page 102*
*Chronic Fatigue Syndrome* ....................................................... *Page 103*
*Leslie Leaves Again* .................................................................. *Page 106*
*Pool Ministry* ........................................................................... *Page 107*
*Jail/Drinking/Drugs* .................................................................. *Page 109*

# TABLE OF CONTENTS

**CHAPTER 7: FLORIDA** -- *RONDO/Quick-Verse/Duet & Chorus*
*Amanda's Miracle And Mine (Heart Tumor)* .................................. *Page 111*
*Deaf Ministry Ends – 5 Books* ....................................................... *Page 118*
*Donna* .............................................................................................. *Page 119*
*Too Good To Be True* ...................................................................... *Page 121*
*Intimacy With God* .......................................................................... *Page 123*
*Tell Your Story* ................................................................................. *Page 126*
*Car Pit Crew* ................................................................................... *Page 136*
*Pageants* .......................................................................................... *Page 137*
*The Grill Room* ................................................................................ *Page 139*

**CHAPTER 8: THE ENCORE – THE NEXT 12 YEARS**
*Deaf Ministry - A New Beginning* .................................................. *Page 142*
*Issue Of Blood* ................................................................................. *Page 143*

**CHAPTER 9: FINALE – NOT YET**
*The Composer Is Still Writing* ........................................................ *Page 147*

# INTRODUCTION

God lead me to write about my life to be a help to others, especially women. To let you know you are not the only one to go through problems and that with God all things are possible. You can make it!

I share struggles with loneliness and planning my own suicide while being a friend, and a listening ear to others. Yet feeling I had no one to turn to.

I followed God's call to be a missionary to the deaf in Jamaica. I saw lives of the deaf changed and have worked with the deaf for over 40 years.

I dealt with failure and being a disappointment to God, the ministry, my church, and my family.

I tell how my daughter and I walked in faith through many life struggles.

I share how I raised my child in church and always believed and trusted God no matter what - praise the Lord Anyhow.

I saw God answer prayer in the lives of my family members while I was growing up. (brother had polio/sister had encephalitis)

God spared my life 4 times. All 4 times Doctors told me I could have or should have died: Mononucleosis, Chronic Fatigue Syndrome, a rare tumor in my heart, and a blood problem (issue) that doctors could not explain. But God miraculously "touched" me and restored my health.

I share how getting and losing jobs along the way have been stepping stones on my journey. Each one was a new movement/song that influenced my life. If I had not lost some I would not have advanced from those places in my life.

I describe relationships that I had, such expectations, and how that I was hurt and disappointed by people/men time and again.

# INTRODUCTION

I explain how God formed me from childhood till now, making me the LifeSong that he wants me to be. I tell how God directed me through life, to locations, and different churches to create this story, **LifeSong – My Symphony**.

I relate my life to a song, a symphony orchestrated by God to reach the hearts of others through the good times and bad times, blessings and struggles. Hence the book: "**LifeSong - My Symphony**". Now God wants me to share my story through the songs he has given me in life.

*My story is intended to help others facing some of the same situations in life.*

My life has been filled with music:

- I started out at 10 years old playing the pipe organ in the Lutheran church
- I accompanied groups from grade school through college
- I played for all the school musicals
- I completed degrees at Baptist bible College and Southwest Missouri State University - piano and music composition. I earned my Masters Degree in Education – music and Deaf Education.
- I played piano, keyboards, even trombone in churches all my life.
- When I reached life's "graduate school", Faithworld, God instructed me to just worship!

# LIFESONG - MY SYMPHONY

# CHAPTER 1: IN REGARDS TO WORK

## *No Job*

The second week of January 1998, I was feeling very low because I had not yet received full-time work and had been out of a full-time job for a little over a year. I thought that I would spend some time in prayer and consideration as to what I should be doing, what jobs I should be looking for and how I should be applying since nothing had happened in the previous year's search. I was working part time, one day a week. Monday I thought, starting tomorrow I am going to spend four days in an extensive time of prayer and fasting to seek God's will for my life from this point on.

I got up that Tuesday morning and started in bible study and prayer, listening to worship tapes and just talking to the Lord. All of a sudden I felt God saying to me to fast until He gives me a full-time job and I said "yea, right, sure", I just spent over a year without a full-time job and I thought this could go another year. Who knows how long? I thought God would really have to supernaturally sustain me or I could get very thin (maybe not a bad thing). I was not really trusting and believing.

I thought, "No", I can't really believe God is telling me to do that because I didn't have anything to look at to convince me that I would have a job any time soon. I continued on in prayer and study and began thinking about different scriptures that deal with fasting. I thought, well, maybe God is trying to tell me that within 40 days I am going to have a full-time job. So I continued in worship and debate with God. Finally I said, "Okay God, what is it you are telling me to do?" I trusted God enough and knew He didn't want me to fast until He gave me a full-time job **unless** He was going to give it to me, within the 40 days or so.

I kept debating with myself and God, kept thinking that was what God wanted me to do and commit to. Finally, I agreed. I thought, okay, if that is what I believe God wants me to do I will just begin today, not just a 40 day fast, but until God tells me to stop or gives me a full-time job.

I continued in prayer and worship and began thinking God would have me tell somebody about this to help hold me accountable. It would be a lot easier to slip if I hadn't told anyone that I was going to do this. I thought if I slip it would just be me and God and I could make some sort of an excuse with God. I had a friend's name come to mind, a lady from my church. I got up and headed to the telephone to let her know I made this commitment between God and myself. I walked toward the telephone, and as I was walking towards the phone it began to ring.

I answered it and it was my part time job (Security Shopper) calling me to see if I would like to go full-time (Uniformed/costumed Security) the following Monday? Naturally I thought I should accept this position but I asked them if I could pause for just a moment and make a phone call which they agreed to do. So I called my church and spoke to one of the elders and got a confirmation that they believed that this is what I should do also. I shared with him what my morning had been like as I had been talking with the Lord and studying.

God graciously granted me a full-time position. I saw once again how God many times just wants us to believe in Him and trust in Him and take Him at his Word as He does provide everything that we need and gives us all the things He says he will. We have to believe Him and trust Him. I sometimes (not that I doubted God and didn't think He could do it) just didn't make that commitment to trust God and believe in Him to do it. Once I made the commitment and understood in my heart and mind that I would do what I believed God wanted me to do, He answered immediately. I didn't have to fast but a moment. That was the shortest fast and time in prayer in my entire life – probably in history. So believe in God, trust Him for all He can do.

I started the job the next Monday with a friend of mine who had also worked with me at the part time job. We both went full-time on the same day. We went through the training and my first assignment my very first day was to the Indy 200 races at Disney. It was pouring down rain and I was assigned to the credentials trailer. My post was to stand outside the trailer and watch people coming and going, to make sure they were the people that were supposed to be there, make sure there were no problems, and assist people in finding their way. It was a frustrating day because of the weather but I grinned and I bore it.

I had several frustrating moments in my first few weeks. Now that I had to wear a costume, getting the right size wasn't easy. My permanent post had every size of female costumes except the one that I needed. It took me over two weeks to get into a costume that actually fit properly. Actually it was over a month until I got everything complete. So those were some of the minor frustrations, things that go along with any job. I wondered why God put me into this kind of job – nothing I was trained in or schooled for. I knew it was not something I felt I would be doing for any length of time.

After a few months on the full-time job, a job opened that was something that I had been interested in for a couple of years. Because I was a full-time employee I was able to apply for that job in the same company. I had a fantastic interview and they assured me in the interview that this would be awesome for me. They asked why I didn't apply for this before (I had) and they gave me a longer interview than normal.

They were really encouraging me and said they would recommend me for two jobs that were open and that I would probably have my choice of the one I really wanted. Then I began another time of waiting on the Lord, I waited a couple of weeks but heard nothing from them, no job offer, no job rejection, and no announcement of who may have gotten the job. I trusted God. He knew whether he wanted me there or not. One thing I had found on this particular job as I was working on patrol in the various areas, I had many opportunities to thank God for the area, silently pray for the people, and bless the area. I believed that was something that God wanted me to do.

I am now going to go back to my first working days in the late 1960s. I had graduated from high school and I had begun nursing school. I found out very quickly that was not the place for me. I flunked out of school. Nursing was the career my father wanted for me. I liked emergency medical work but did not like all the in hospital stuff.

## *First Job - Telephone Company*

I then found myself looking for a much-needed job. I was a Christian and was praying about a job and was asking God what he would have me to do. A neighbor lady who was a guidance counselor at a high school told me about opportunities at Ohio Bell. She had a connection there with someone in the Human Resources Department and sent me down to apply. I was hired. My first full-time job was to work for the telephone company as a directory assistance operator (back in the days when we looked everything up in the books, before the time everything was computerized).

They still had the old cord boards for long-distance when I began working there. I had a good time working there, made a lot of friends, shared with people my testimony and my church, and became a witness. I felt God wanted me there during the days of his preparing me for something else.

I was very active and involved in my church while I worked at Ohio Bell. After two years or so, I became eligible for promotion to supervisor. My first frustrating experience with a job was that I was bypassed on a promotion because I did not wear a girdle. Now don't laugh, this is TRUE. I had a lot of problems with wearing tight things around my middle area so I didn't wear a girdle and I was bypassed for a promotion because of that.

This was back in the days before women were allowed to wear slacks to work. Everyone wore dresses, skirts, and hose and all that fun stuff. I wondered why, why would this happen? I had a good work record and was eligible for the promotion. The union actually jumped in and was checking into it. Not at my request but simply because it was not a proper decision.

## *Jamaica*

Before that request issue was resolved, I had taken a trip to Jamaica, West Indies. There I felt God's call to the mission field (which I share in another chapter of this book). At that time I felt I would leave the

Telephone Company and go to work on the mission field in Jamaica. I trusted God and started going around to churches to raise support for the mission field. I had now worked for 2 years and 9 months at the phone company. To go to the mission field, I would have no definite financial security, only what people would send me from the states. People thought I was crazy for giving up that job with the phone company because, after all, "that is a lifetime security and you don't want to give that up".

I had a lot of people try to discourage me because they felt I was giving up such a good job and good career. They thought it was kind of neat that I wanted to go but yet, you know… and yet there were others who were surprised and delighted that I wanted to do this. It was great testimony to those that I worked with, that I was willing to give up the security, good pay, and everything. I had my own apartment and things were going quite well financially for me. In fact I had just bought a new car. I was willing to give all that up to follow God's leading to the mission field. I went from Ohio to Jamaica.

## *Church Secretary*

Upon my return from Jamaica 2 years later, when my daughter was a few months old, I began working at my church as a church secretary. My pastors were very involved in Christian radio and the development of Christian radio. I got to do some things with that as well. I worked between the church and the radio station doing several projects for the pastors.

One day while I was sitting in the church office doing my work I received a call from Ohio Bell Telephone Company. I had reapplied to the telephone company after returning from Jamaica.

## *Telephone Company – My Mission Field*

I returned at that time to work for the telephone company which continued for a total of 18 years. I worked several years there in Canton, Ohio.

# LIFESONG - MY SYMPHONY

I packed up everything I owned in my little Buick Skylark, took my daughter who was now almost two years old, and we moved to Springfield, Missouri. I drove into town, bought a newspaper, and started calling for places to live. I found a little apartment. We had a little old lady next door that we called Granny. She babysat every day for her daughter's son. We got to talking and before the weekend was over, she had agreed to baby-sit for Leslie while I worked and went to Bible school.

That began a 15 year stay in Springfield. With the years at the phone company in Springfield, Missouri added to what I had worked for the phone company in Ohio, I had worked a total of 18 years between Ohio Bell, Southwestern Bell and AT&T (through divestiture Southwestern Bell became AT&T). Many, many times my work was a mission field for me. As people would come in feeling down, having a hurt, or wanting to share praise, they would often seek me out to sit beside. They knew that I was someone they could share with or that they could come to if they had a prayer need or family need. So I used it as a place to be a witness and a testimony for God and I prayed that God would continue to use me there and keep me there as long as he needed me to minister there.

Eventually, the divestiture caught up to us and they were going to be closing the office I worked in. They offered a buy-out which I took because the only options were to move to Kansas City or Tulsa, Oklahoma. I did not want to go to either one so I just went ahead and accepted the buy-out. During the years I was there with AT&T, I worked as an operator. I worked the directory assistance and then worked my way into what they called the TSP (traffic service positions) operator. I eventually became a relief supervisor and an acting manager (without the girdle).

I had done a lot and worked my way up in the company through the years I was there. However, there was no opportunity for full time management because of the divestiture. They said it would be years because of all the downsizing that was coming.

It turns out, as I look back now, they were correct. There were many of us who were affected by divestiture that had been approved for management. I had been assessed very high for management but had no opportunities to become a permanent manager.

I appreciated all those years with the telephone company and all the benefits it provided. Because of the solid income I earned there, I was able to raise my daughter and provide for her a home and things that a growing child needs. I had a good time working there and made a lot of good friends who I truly love and appreciate.

## *Teaching*

As I attended Baptist Bible College, my work and background with the deaf became known. I began teaching Sign Language and Interpreting at the Baptist Bible College. I ended up doing that for 11 years as well as being a supply teacher in the music program. So for 11 of those years that I was with the phone company I was part time teaching at the college which I very dearly enjoyed. I really liked working with the college age students and appreciated being able to teach them.

I also began teaching at Sonshine Performing Arts Academy in Springfield where my daughter was a student. That is where she studied dance and modeling. I began teaching piano, keyboard, and voice at Sonshine. Through all my years, all my life, from the time I was very young, I was teaching someone piano, occasionally voice and various things with music and choir and so on.

The teacher in me was always alive as I worked in other jobs as well as teaching at Baptist Bible College. After finishing Baptist Bible College, I went on to Southwest Missouri State University and earned several degrees in education in both the music and the deaf education fields. I also began substitute teaching in the Springfield public schools and taught in the deaf-education and music classes there.

I was active in the classroom the day of the Challenger explosion. We watched the television coverage throughout the day in my classroom. Later, after moving to Titusville, Florida, I was there when they had the first shuttle flight after the Challenger accident. I am very sentimental, so it was a very meaningful thing to me that I was able to be a part of it as the shuttle program took off again.

# LIFESONG - MY SYMPHONY

After all of those years of working at AT&T, going to college, raising Leslie, and teaching on the side, I took the buy-out from AT&T and then wondered, "Lord what should I do?" Should I continue in substitute teaching or should I teach private piano and voice? Just what should I do?

We had made a visit to Florida to visit my brother and he suggested that we move to the Orlando, Florida, area. While Leslie and I were thinking over what we should do and contemplating the move, my brother said that there were many people in his church that he had told about me and they felt like I would be an asset to their church music ministry. They began praying for me to find a job in Florida. I believe that the people from that church prayed me to Florida.

**Many of these jobs/experiences will be referred to again in this book as I take you on the journey of my LifeSong.**

# CHAPTER 2: CHILDHOOD

## Family

Meyersdale, Pennsylvania is a small town in the hills of Somerset County, Pennsylvania. That is where I was born. I used to love the place, the small town, the atmosphere, my friends there, the neighborhood. It was all something that was very special to me in my childhood. My father had served in the U.S. Army during WWII and was working with his father at the bakery. My grandfather owned the bakery in town. It was known as *Twigg's Bakery*.

Often as I grew older I would spend days, particularly Saturdays, occasionally with my father. He had to be there between 4:00-5:00 in the morning to open up the place and I would go in and help them, help as a child does. They started baking the bread in the morning. I used to watch my father decorate cakes and make the cookies and cinnamon rolls and all the good things you find in a bakery. It was a wonderful smelling place. I learned a lot there about baking.

I remember my first experience with a rat was in the back of the bakery, back by the big flour bin. As I walked back to get something for my dad this huge black thing ran out in front of me. I squealed of course. Dad said it came in from the alley. Later I learned about trapping and getting rid of rats and mice, as well as other critters.

SIDENOTE: *I also learned that people can sometimes be like rats or pests in our life. The trick is learning how and when to get them out of your life.*

Cooking I learned from my mother at home. She cooked meals every day and I learned from her. By the age of 12, I was doing a lot of cooking at home for our family. By that time my father had taken a job traveling and selling. He was selling bakery supplies to bakeries around the area. My mother would go to open and close the bakery every day. I was at home with my younger brothers and sister and I would do the cooking in the evening a lot of times. I learned to cook and bake and clean and all those things at a young age.

My mother was from a neighboring community and a very large family. They grew up on a farm outside of a little town called Friedens, Pennsylvania. I used to love to go there and visit my grandmother's home. My grandfather had died before I was born so I never knew him. My grandmother lived out in the country on a farm and many times through the years my mother and all of her 8 living sisters and 1 brother would get together there at the home place. I had 30 something first cousins and we would have these wonderful times meeting together and playing together and getting to know each other. It was always a lot of fun and I grew very close to our family ties.

My grandparents on my father's side lived just 2 doors down the street from us. I was very close to them as well. I would go from my house to their house daily. Our houses were located on a hillside with a creek flowing at the bottom (Flockerty Creek). On the hillside between the creek and the houses many people would have gardens and my grandfather had a very huge garden. I would go over there often during the summertime and pick certain vegetables that we would use for meals and cooking on that day. I liked to be out there in things of nature.

I spent one day out there in the garden picking some vegetables and I thought I heard someone calling my name. I looked around and saw no one. I often felt like I was sitting there and that at a young age felt God was calling out to me for something. I did not know what or where, why or how, but I just felt like God was calling me.

My father had 3 sisters but I only had 7 first cousins on that side of the family. I saw them often as well. There were many holiday gatherings at Grandma & Grandpa Twigg's. They both played the piano and loved to sing hymns.

On my mother's side of the family I had one of my aunts and uncles with 7 children that lived on a farm. I used to like to go there every summer and spend a week or two. I would ride with them on the hay wagon as they would be bailing the hay. Again I loved the nature and the farm, the animals, the growing of the crops and it was something I enjoyed very much as a child.

## *Camp Sequanota*

Another one of my fondest childhood memories was the camp I used to go to. We went to a Lutheran church and my parents were very faithful. Every Sunday they took us to church and from an early age I started going to church camp. I ended up going to Camp Sequanota yearly for about 10 years. I loved the nature hikes and those early morning walks with a devotion time. We would go out and were supposed to find ourselves our own little spot. I loved being out in the woods.

The morning devotions were one of the first real experiences where I found myself having a close, intimate, time with God. I would take my Bible and the study materials they had given us and I took it very seriously. I would go out on those mornings and spend the time with God in devotion. That was my first introduction to spending quiet time, private time alone with God, studying his words and talking with him, expecting God to hear and answer. I enjoyed that camp. Like I said, I went back for 10 years.

However, that first year there they had just put in a regular swimming pool. Up until that time the campers had done their swimming in the lake. They had a brand new swimming pool and everybody had thought that was just so wonderful. I went there with very long blonde hair. They were starting to have swimming pools built around the country. Working with the chemicals and all was new and they didn't have things quite right yet. I loved the swimming pool and spent a lot of time there through the week. I couldn't understand my mother's shock when they came to pick me up from camp.

Of course, I had spent a lot of time in the pool but I had also showered everyday and washed my hair but little did I realize, not even particularly noticing in the mirror, that my hair had drastically changed color. It was no longer this nice, light, whitish blonde but now a very dark, dull, greenish color. So when I left the camp that year the camp directors and owners were fearful that I would never return and they were not sure what my parents would think when they saw my hair. However, like I said, I did come back. I remember going home and my mother putting me in the bathtub and washing my hair many, many times. It kept coming out green and for six months we were washing that stuff out of my hair. Of course, my hair began turning darker and never was that white golden blonde again.

Camp was an interesting experience. We had classes each day. Besides the Bible studies, learning things about God, and the nature experiences, I felt myself even as a child drawing close to God and wanting to know more about him. I wanted to be closer to God and experience more of him.

## *Church - Music*

In the Lutheran church we had a good pastor and our family went to church all the time. We were always involved in all the activities and I began singing in the children's choir. That was one of my first musical experiences. I really liked being involved in the children's choir at church. Some of the very first songs I remember singing are *"Ivory Palaces"* and *"Jacob's Ladder"*.

One Halloween I was in 3rd grade. It was Halloween night and back in those days we all got dressed up and went trick or treating. There was no problem going throughout the neighborhood through the whole town trick or treating because that is what everybody did. Nobody had ever heard of or talked about satanic influence involved with Halloween. We just knew it was a fun time to get dressed up and go get candy and see all the neighbors and friends. This particular Halloween was no different. We had gotten dressed. I remember my brother and I were ready to go out and there was a knock on the door.

When I answered the door it was the delivery of a piano. I will never forget that Lester piano as it was delivered that night. I didn't want to go out trick or treating. I just wanted to stay home and play with this new thing that they had brought into our home. That became the love affair of my life and from that day on I began spending many, many hours a day at this instrument.

# LIFESONG - MY SYMPHONY

I started taking piano lessons. My piano teacher belonged to my church and she was very thrilled to have me as a student because unlike many, I was very interested in the instrument and spent hours each week practicing and doing exactly what she would tell me to do and more.

I was eight years old when I first got the piano. The church was just having a pipe organ installed at that time (one of the biggest pipe organs in the country). So even though I was very young, my teacher began giving me instruction on the pipe organ. By age 10 I was playing for services at church. They didn't have enough people to play the organ at two services each Sunday. We had an early service and a later service. So I began playing for the earlier services at age 10. I enjoyed doing that very much and really enjoyed that instrument. It taught me so much. It taught me about different sounds and different backgrounds, how to choose settings, how to get involved with the instrument you are playing. I really cherish those years there.

They did not have enough people to play the piano so at that same young age I began playing the piano for the men's Sunday school class. I did not realize these were things adults normally did. I was doing these things at age 10 and 11. I realized much later that God was teaching me to draw close to him through my music and as I played and practiced, not only on the church music, but as I began studying the classical music and playing things like Clair de lune.

Clair de lune became my favorite and it remains one of my most favorite pieces. I love to play that piece. I feel so close to God through it. I feel like Claude Debussy, whether he knew God or not, had to have had some sort of closeness to God to get the sounds and the feelings he expressed in his music. He wrote a lot about things in nature which were things that were close to me as well. I just sense and feel all of that through his music.

I enjoy playing various types of music but the one piece that has remained my favorite through all these years is Clair de lune. And I still reach a peak of drawing close to God as I play that song and as I climb through those notes I feel like I am reaching to the mountaintop and ascending there to meet God and fellowship with him through the instrument.

So that was my beginning in music.

## *Meyersdale*

Meyersdale, Pennsylvania, is a small town and in those years everybody left their houses unlocked. You didn't have to worry about people coming in. You only locked it if you were going away for a couple of days or something. You just would go out and shut the door and that was it. You didn't have to worry about anybody going in or doing anything in your home while you were gone.

I went to school in the town and we walked to school. I remember walking up a hill to go to the younger grades and then I remember after 4th grade beginning to walk over town to school. I remember one particular morning I got up and it was snowing very heavily and there was deep snow outside. That was before girls could wear slacks to school. You had to wear dresses or skirts. But you were allowed to wear slacks or leggings underneath and I was all bundled up in all these warm clothes, boots and scarves and it was snowing so hard. I started out and climbed up the hill. The wind was blowing and snow was falling fast. I didn't see anybody. Nobody was out. I wondered what was happening.

I was probably in 5th grade. I got all the way over to the school which was some distance away and I met a janitor. He said that there is no school today; school has been called off because of the snow. For some reason that particular morning my mother wasn't listening to the radio like she normally did so I didn't know school had been called off. I was one of few, if not the only one who showed up that morning. So then I traveled back home in the snow again and made it back home safely.

Those are the types of things I remember from my childhood.

I was also a Girl Scout. We had evening meetings and I remember I would walk (again no problems with going out and walking alone or with another friend at night even though we were only 8, 9, 10 years old).

One of the things we liked to do traveling back and forth was to play a little game with the parking meters. Of course our uniform was a skirt but we would practice leap-frog over the parking meters on our way to Girl Scouts. I enjoyed Girl Scouts very much and feel like all those things were very important to me in my formative years.

One other thing that took place in Meyersdale was the Maple Festival. Meyersdale is in the area where the maple sap runs fluid and it's a big area for maple syrup and all those yummy things that are made out of the maple syrup. Meyersdale became the home of the Maple Festival. I used to love to go and see the girls compete for the title of queen of the maple festival. I guess that was my beginning in pageants.

When I was in first grade I was one of the people selected to be a little princess for the Maple Festival that year. My mother said I used to embarrass her because I had all this pretty blonde hair and everyone thought I was so cute. I can't imagine that, I never saw myself that way – then or now. But I was selected to be one of the little princesses and it made me feel so special. I knew I was going to grow up and become the big Maple Festival Queen when I was a senior in high school. That was going to be my thing. Of course many things changed between then and the time I got to be a senior in high school. But it has remained a very wonderful and pleasant memory. I often think back to the days of the Maple Festival.

Our neighbors were all very close. Our neighbors on one side owned a big business in town. Every year for the Maple Festival there was a parade and a lot of the businesses in the area would put a float into the parade. Even after that first grade experience for many years I was involved in helping them make the float and often got to ride on the float. We would put flowers on and papier-mâché. They were quite fun days around the Maple Festival each year. It is still a big event taking place yearly. Meyersdale really comes alive at the Maple Festival time.

Another thing that I remember fondly was our front porch. I loved to go out on the porch. There was a little cover over the top, it was not netted in or anything but it had a roof on it and we had a swing. I really enjoyed going out there and swinging in the evening.

# LIFESONG - MY SYMPHONY

I remember storms...I used to like to go out there during storms to watch the lightening and listen to the thunder. I would count the seconds from the time I saw the lightening until I heard the thunder. That would tell me how many miles away the lightening was. I remember my father liked to do that too. He would go out there with me. My mother didn't like storms so she would stay inside. But my father and I would go out on the porch and watch as the storms were taking place.

I remember a time standing on the porch (I was in 3rd or 4th grade) and my father saying to me, "What do you want to do when you grow up?" I really didn't even have to think about it. I said I want to be a medical missionary. I didn't have any idea at that time that I would eventually become a missionary, sort of as a medical missionary. I would become a missionary and involved in some medical things through the years. It was kind of a foreshadowing I guess of things to come.

Outside in the street was where the neighborhood kids would gather. In those days we weren't afraid to play in the middle of the street because once everybody was home from work there was very little traffic. We would go out in the middle of the street and play a game called Kick the Can. It was before we had computers or any of those fantastic electronics we have today. We would go out there and take a simple can and play, Kick the Can. There was a little girl down the street, her name was Donna, she and I would play together: building blocks and dolls. The doll of the age was the Jenny doll and we both had Jenny dolls. We would get together and dress and play with our Jenny dolls.

Our next door neighbor was Jerry. You remember I told you about being on the hillside with the creek at the bottom. A lot of the driveways would go from the top before the houses, down past the gardens, by the creek. Some of them had sheds built at the very bottom. Well, we would go over to Jerry's driveway in the winter time and take our sleds and sled ride down this hill. Oh what fun...! I used to love to sled ride, especially head first. I would jump on that thing and go head first. However, one year they had put a rock pile at the bottom so that if any of us couldn't turn we wouldn't go into the creek. I guess they didn't consider the fact that we could have been in just as much trouble if we hit the pile of rocks which I did. I lost control of my sled one time and went head first into the rocks. I had to go have stitches put in my head.

We had a swing set built in the backyard and I walked too close one time when someone was on the swing and they hit me right in the corner of the eye and I had some stitches there too! So my childhood, as you can see, was what I considered to be normal at the time.

We also had a cherry tree in the backyard. Jerry was king of the tree. He always went to the highest limb and he was the king, and that was his spot. One time when he wasn't there I was going to show him that I could get up there too. Of course I was a little shorter and not quite as long legged, not quite as old either. I climbed up there. I pulled and I struggled and got to Jerry's limb. However, I could not get back down. Ultimately, when Jerry's father eventually came home he realized I was in the tree. He had to get a ladder to get me out of the tree.

These are just a few of my childhood memories I wanted to share with you so you would know a little bit about what has formed me.

I had another girlfriend that lived just up the street from me. Amazingly enough, her name was Karen and she became my best friend. Many of my best friends through the years have been named Karen. She and I became very good friends. We were the same age, went to the same school, lived within a block and a half of each other and played together all the time. We became very, very close. And then two other children moved into our neighborhood and they were Patty and Dick. They were the new high school principal's children. We all became good friends and we all spent many hours and many days together in each other's houses, yards and developing these good close friendships.

I had a brother that was born when I was 4 years old. When he was 2 years old (I was 6 years old) he got polio. I remember as we were standing there and they were telling us what he had and they didn't expect him to live. This was during the days of the polio epidemic. He became extremely ill, completely paralyzed, and couldn't swallow.

# LIFESONG - MY SYMPHONY

I remember standing on the little step stool in our kitchen as they were talking about this disease. The rest of the family needed to have polio vaccinations. My brother might die. I remember my parents talking about prayer and believing in God. That was all still very new to me. They took my brother away to a hospital and he ended up gone from us for two years being put into a couple of different hospitals. He finally did recover from the polio and got back some of his movements in parts of his body. Through the years he had to have various surgeries and different things would affect his life.

I remember that they put him into a home for crippled children in Pittsburgh Pennsylvania. It was about ninety miles east of where we lived so every weekend we would make the trip to Pittsburgh and go visit my brother. Even though I was very young (6-8 years old) that started touching my heart for other people that I would see and meet.

I remember some of the children. How my heart just reached out to them so much because they were left there and no one came to visit them. No one seemed to care about them. They had become ill or disabled and their families just left them. It just broke my heart to see and know that there were people that no one really seemed to care about and such young children. God put it in my heart at a very early age a concern and a compassion for people who didn't have things like I did and who weren't as complete and whole as I was, people who had been abandoned or seemed to be abandoned by others.

My younger brother and sister were born a few years later. They were 18 months apart and my brother was about 4 years old at the time they were born. Things were also changing at the bakery and my father became a salesman. I began helping mother at home with the cooking and cleaning and things like that.

We had another neighbor that was my mother's best friend. Her name was Ruthie. She was a great cook and always kept us laughing. Her husband Monee worked for the railroad. Monee took to my brother Kevin. He would take Kevin on train rides with him. Kevin still loves trains.

# Chapter 3: MY YOUTH

## Ohio – I Accepted The Free Gift Of Salvation

At the age of 12, my family decided to move to Ohio. My father's job selling supplies to bakeries had changed and his territory was moved to the Ohio area. We were required to move to Ohio. This was a very traumatic time for me. I had just completed 6th grade, was getting ready to go into junior high and high school, and was involved in many activities. Like I said, it was a small neighborhood. I knew everybody, and I was settled into everything I did there, plus being close to all the cousins, the family. When I knew that we were going to be moving it was very hard for me because I did not want to go. But of course I had no choice.

We moved in August of 1960 to Massillon, Ohio, to an area called Perry Heights. We moved into a house that was on a corner that had wooded land behind it and across the street from it. I was at least thankful for that because it reminded me somewhat of Pennsylvania. I began meeting people and making friends at school.

My family started looking for a church home and in the first several weeks that we were there we visited many different churches. In one of the visits we went to the Massillon Baptist Temple. The preacher got up that morning, gave a sermon, and gave an invitation at the close of that service.

I had seen invitations when I had visited the Brethren church with my grandma and grandpa Twigg. I was a little bit familiar with some of those things. But I had heard that message and knew it was for me. I made a decision that day and my decision was to accept the free gift of salvation that Jesus Christ was offering me and to accept the fact that he had died and shed his blood in my place on that cross of eternity. So at 12 years of age I went forward to the invitation that was given at the close of the service. Later I realized that those years of learning and preparation in the Lutheran church had done everything to prepare me

# LIFESONG - MY SYMPHONY

to hear that message and be saved. The Lutheran training brought me to the point of salvation. I was ready for it.

My family kept visiting churches and finally decided to attend the church called The Peoples Church. It was a very strong influence on my life and I realize how God put me there and every location I have been in and every church I have been involved in because he had special things for me to learn in each place. I really enjoyed the music. It was upbeat. They had piano and organ all the time, a nice big choir, and a couple hundred people in the congregation. The pastor was very enthusiastic and energetic and his son worked as an associate pastor. We started attending there and I became very involved in Sunday school.

As a child in the Lutheran church I had had a Sunday school teacher for many years who was very thorough and very good in teaching and explaining things in the scripture. So now I continued and built on the foundation from the Lutheran church.

I had many wonderful Sunday school teachers through the years, particularly one lady that worked with us 3-4 years during my high school years. She was one of the main leaders in the youth group and was very influential on my life; to the extent that after I graduated from high school I began working with her and working with the youth within a year or so after my leaving the youth department myself. It was very fulfilling to me.

I also had many wonderful music experiences there. It was very exciting. The assistant pastor started what he called Cantons Great Sunday Night Crusade and we had crusade type services every Sunday evening. My pastor and his son were very instrumental in developing the Christian radio network that we know today. They had started in the Canton area just broadcasting, being on the air. Then they developed a station that put all Christian broadcasting on that station. Then they started reaching out to other radio stations and other pastors across the country and eventually developed into this fantastic network reaching out all across the country.

The pastor told us that he had a vision of reaching all these millions of people and didn't understand how God was going to work that and use that in his life. But later, with all the developments of radio, he realized how that vision God had given him had come to pass. It was teaching me that we are to trust ideas and dreams that God gives us; And that in his way and his day and his time he brings those things to pass (this book for example). In many ways we don't know or don't understand or know what they mean when we first have these thoughts and visions. I learned those kinds of principles through the teaching of the pastor and the leadership in that church.

## *High School Days*

In my high school years I made many friends. There was a trio of girls that became my best friends. They were Peggy, Patty and Joan. We did many things together. We played in the band. We rode the same school bus to school because we lived in the same area and had gone to the same Edison Jr. High and Perry High School together. We shared many things. I invited them many times to go to church with me. I went to church with them. We shared many growing experiences through our teen years.

As they started dating, I didn't as much, but as they did, we would be all girls and have girl talks about their relationships and their boyfriends and all of those things that girls do. We were 'Normal Teenagers'. As we continued together through school, we learned to drive together. I was the first one to get my driver's license. I remember our first night out. We were going to a band function and I was to pick up the girls and take them. It was an exciting adventure as I ran over the curb (several times). So those kinds of memories we shared together.

I remember sharing with them from time to time my beliefs in Christ and my beliefs in church. I know at various times throughout our relationship some of them made decisions for Christ as well. It was fulfilling to me as I began to see people that I was sharing with and talking with make decisions for Christ in their own life.

One of the most traumatic things in my youth was when one of these girl's sister was killed in an automobile accident, an accident which occurred right in front of my church. It was a very nasty accident, a head on collision and the girl's sister and her sister's fiancé were both killed instantly in this accident. My father at the time volunteered on emergency medical crews and he was out there but didn't even realize who it was at the time.

I remember receiving a call from my friend early the next morning and realizing the girl had been killed and the things and circumstances surrounding it. How the boy's parents didn't approve of their relationship and so after the accident they didn't contact her parents at all during the time of the funerals and remorse. Her parents decided to bury her (Karen was her name) in her wedding dress because all she had dreamed about was getting married and looking forward to life with this young man.

Ironically enough, it turned out that the two of them were buried without the parents consulting one another or knowing what was going on in the funeral arrangements, the young man and young woman ended up buried head to head in the same cemetery. I thought it was ironic how God puts us together in life and death. I know that was something that greatly influenced me in my youth as I was looking at that situation and wondering how it was orchestrated and how it happened that way. Not understanding why some people in their youth, so young and vivacious, could have their lives snuffed out, learning that we don't always know what God's purpose is.

Shortly after we moved to Ohio my sister became very ill. She was four years old. She was taken to the hospital with very high temperatures. And of course, I remembered going through things with my brother a few years earlier. It turned out she had encephalitis. She had partial paralysis and again it was a situation where we didn't know if she was going to live or die. Again I heard my parents talking about praying and I saw them seek God. I did too.

This time I was a little older understood a little bit more. Again I saw God work miraculously as he brought my sister back to life and restored her. She had some problems as a result through the years as well but God was so good to restore her life and he answered the cry out from my parents, me, other relatives, church family, and others, as we reached out in prayer during that time.

During those years, my brother was going to school and my parents were very determined to give him public schooling. He started school in Pennsylvania and then continued in Ohio. It was before all the mandatory things were in place for people with handicaps and they were encouraging my parents to put my brother into a school that was for handicapped people. The problem was that the school contained children with handicaps of all kinds but particularly mentally handicapped students. My parents insisted that he had no problems mentally and felt that it would hold him back because his problems were physical. He didn't have the mobility but he had the mentality. So they agreed in the early days to allow him to go to public school if my parents would transport him. He started in regular public school and of course he followed me into high school.

We both played trombone in the band. An outstanding thing was that he became involved in the high school band, even the marching band. They would march out into the field into formation. He could not march with them but once they were in formation he would walk out with his canes and trombone and play with them. Then he would walk off the field and the band would march off. Eventually he made a trip with the School Band of America to Europe and went on to college.

That was my first realization that we often stereotype and label people with a disability or a handicap and don't really give them the opportunity to go and grow on their own. God put that in my heart as I saw my brother accomplish things. Had my parents followed all the advice that was given, my brother would have not had the advantages of physically or mentally achieving the things he did in life. So I am grateful for the heart that God put into my parents. They taught me so many things that I would use later in life. I learned to have a heart and compassion for people if I see them struggling. I realize they can have opportunities and abilities if we just give them the opportunities to use and develop those abilities.

## *Music, Music, Music*

I stayed involved in piano and organ music through my youth. I started with another teacher after moving to Ohio and, because of the way I could play, she assumed I knew many things that I actually did not know such as understanding chords. I could sight read very well and play rhythms and so she thought I had a basic understanding of chording. She started marking all these things in my music. She would call off chords and I had no idea what she was talking about. But I would still come back and play it because I could read it on the music or heard it when it was demonstrated for me. It became frustrating for me because I struggled to understand everything she was talking about.

I continued playing the piano and developed the ability to play many different styles of music, particularly church music. I quickly became an assistant pianist at church and if someone was absent they would use me to fill in. It was the pastor's wife who played the organ and another woman played the piano. Then later the pastor's son, who was the assistant pastor, married a woman who played the piano and she became the pianist. I remained the substitute when someone was gone from the piano or organ. When I was in high school I started directing the children's choir and directing the youth choir. I stayed very involved musically as I grew up.

I remember just waiting for the day. You had to be a freshman in high school to join the adult choir at church. I couldn't wait for the days to pass so that I would be of age where I could be a part of that choir. It was something I so much wanted to be a part of. Through the years, we sang for all the special occasions, cantatas, and many special events.

Because of my church being involved in the radio ministry, I met many of the people we heard on the radio. They were very popular Christian radio speakers and pastors. They would come to our church and be guest speakers, sometimes for just the day, sometimes for a week and sometimes even two weeks at a time. And not only speakers, I heard many, many, wonderful bible teachers, preachers throughout the years but also many marvelous musicians.

At that time, the popular thing was the gospel quartets. Many of them came to the church. We also had the Spurlows, the Continentals, Mack Evans, and the Gaithers. There were so many that came. I was so hungry for everything all of them had to say, and for all of their music ministries that meant so much to me. I did not realize that I was on a training ground. God had me there listening to all these people, siphoning what they had to say, taking the scriptures that they shared and putting all that to work in my life's song. I felt God had them there especially for me, to teach me, prepare me, and create me for what he wanted me to be for future service for him. I remember it being a good time, an enjoyable time. I had friends at church and my school buddies that I hung out with regularly, but God was becoming my best friend. I determined and I knew in my heart that God wanted me to stay pure and whole.

Once a year my Youth for Christ leader would take us to Winona Lake, Indiana for the Youth for Christ conference. That was another very special time for me as I would again meet different people, different speakers, different preachers; different song groups, and sing in large choirs under the direction of some of the most fantastic music directors in the world. The trips there were always a lot of fun; we would cook for ourselves and take care of things. I remember at age 15 I was sitting in one of these meetings at Winona Lake. Someone had given a message on God sending us and God calling us out to places of service where God would have us to go.

At the close of his message he said that if you believe God is calling you to surrender to service, go to one of your counselors from your group when you get back to your room where you are staying and share with them and talk with them. They sang that song <u>So Send I You</u>.

I remember at age 15 standing up in that service and, by that, committing myself to God by saying, "Here am I, send me", committing to go wherever He would lead me to go and I would dedicate my life to full time service for God. And then I began from that moment on waiting and wondering for a period of time what God was going to do with me. I felt like I had given my life to God, surrendered my life to Him, but then I began thinking that God must not want to use me because nothing was happening. Of course, not realizing then, that all the things that I was involved with and all the things I was doing were training me for what God was planning and preparing for me in my life.

*Isaiah 6:8 -*
*Also I heard the voice of the Lord saying, Whom shall I send, and who will go for us? Then said I, Here am I; send me.*

## Relationships

Although I did not date yet, I became interested in a boy from church. He was a couple of years older than I was but, still, he was a teenager. My best friend at the time, whose name was Karen by the way, was from my church and we did a lot of things together. She knew that I liked this fellow. He would call me on the telephone and I would talk to him. My father was very strict on dating and because the boy was older, my father didn't want me to have anything to do with him. I wasn't allowed to date. I was only 15. Within the next year or so, things happened. I was 16, Karen was 17, and she knew how I felt about this young man and knew that he had still been calling me. All of a sudden, her engagement was announced. She was to be married to this young man.

Not only that, she asked me to be a bridesmaid in her wedding. I was very hurt by it but by the same token I felt he wasn't for me. I knew I wasn't going to be married that young. So I became her bridesmaid in her wedding but I had felt a loss because I really did like this fellow and would have liked an opportunity to, within another year or two, date him. I didn't feel that any of us should be looking towards marriage at our young age.

There were a couple of different fellows from church through the years that I thought I would like to date or become interested in but again things were very strict at home. For some reason they were never quite good enough, even though they were from the church or from Youth for Christ. They just didn't quite fit the bill. There was another fellow at church that I liked. We would talk occasionally on the telephone or be together at some of the youth activities. He always wanted to play kiss face in the church basement.

I was now a senior in high school and I decided to go into nursing school, not as much because it was something that I really wanted to do, but it was something my parents, especially my father, would like for me to do. And it was something that I had some interest in so I had applied for the nursing school. I had been accepted at Canton Ohio Altman Hospital and was planning to go there in the fall. Another girl from my church, another Karen, was a year ahead of me and had gone to the same high school. We knew each other but hadn't been extremely close. We were involved in some of the same activities at church. She entered that nursing school a year before me so I got to know her more and we became quite good friends.

While at nursing school I started praying with a fellow student. Other students learned about our times of prayer and began to join us. We prayed for many concerns of the girls, our patients, salvation of lost friends, upcoming tests, etc. Some did not have a personal experience with Jesus and we were able to lead them to Christ. That prayer meeting continued for years after I attended the school.

That fellow from church; I can't remember why he had to go into the hospital, appendix or something. Anyway, I went to the hospital to visit him and while I was there he was telling me about this fellow they had brought in the night before that had been in this horrendous motorcycle accident, how tore up he was and what a mess. And that he had been in this motorcycle gang.

I didn't know who it was, but I began to pray for him and then I later realized from my good friend at Youth for Christ that this was someone they had made contact with and apparently after a day or so in the hospital, something happened, he had accepted Christ as his savior and was turning his life completely around. Then he was in the hospital recuperating from this accident. I went with one of my friends from Youth for Christ to visit this young man in the hospital and that began a series of frequent visits to the hospital. I got to know him quite well.

As he was recuperating I would go visit him in the hospital and we would share scriptures, songs, and I learned that he had a heart for people who were involved with delinquency because of the lifestyle he had come from. He was a few years older and he had been through a lot. He had planned after he got out of the hospital (he was there for several weeks) that he was going to become involved with the Youth for Christ organization and work with delinquent teens. This was an area I was interested in as well and so I would probably be working with him at times. He recuperated and got out of the hospital and started that work. As we worked together I became more and more interested in him and I thought I was beginning to fall in love with him. He expressed an interest in me as well. I thought he and I would be together for a lifetime.

He knew from the very beginning that I took a very firm stand on what I believed and what I felt as far as my morality and the Christian stand I was taking. I was fully convinced that I should not have sex before I was married and he respected all of that very much. I appreciated that in him; however, we had some problems with my father. My father knew his background and, for some reason, he couldn't get beyond that. My father had made the statement that he knew what he was like when he was that age and that he didn't want to trust anyone with his daughter.

We had problems for quite a while even though by this time I was 18 years old. I could make up my own mind and make my own decisions on some of those things but I was still living at home until that fall when I went to nursing school.

I started nursing school and things were a little bit strained here and there because of my relationship with my boyfriend. In November of the first year of nursing school they had what they called a capping ceremony and that was when all the new students received their first nurses cap and then each year you would get a stripe to be added onto that cap. I started school and was looking forward to that capping service with excitement. My father had been so proud that I was going to become a nurse and going into that profession but he chose not to come to my capping service. And that was because my boyfriend was coming.

My boyfriend and I were on and off after that. Sometimes, out of respect for my father, we would break off here and there and not see each other for awhile but something would draw us back together. And, because of our involvement at Youth for Christ, we were thrown together a lot. There was also another girl who had been a nurse and someone who had assisted in his care at the hospital who was supposed to be a Christian girl and very interested in him. She called him all the time and tried to get him to go out with her. From time to time he would go out with her and would always tell me about it. I knew that he was seeing her.

There was a young girl that I had known in high school that people didn't want to associate with. She kept coming to my mind. When I was visiting my boyfriend in the hospital he told me about a girl he used to date and that she is from this poor family and that he wanted to go to that family and witness to them, share his salvation. Every time he mentioned her for some reason I would think about the girl I knew in school. So one day when he was out of the hospital and we were working with Youth for Christ, he asked if I would go with him to visit with this family. We pulled up and it was a very old run down house and as we went inside the conditions were very, very poor and very, very dirty, not good conditions.

But much to my amazement the girl that I had reached out to in high school was a sister to the girl that he had dated. We went in and started sharing with the family which started a whole series of visits. I remember going and sitting down with them. The dad would especially like it when we would come and share scripture and share testimonies of things that were happening in our lives. It was a very important time for me to be able to reach out to someone that had been on my mind for a long time as someone that people took advantage of, made fun of, and picked on. I believe God kept her on my mind so that I could reach out to her, share Christ with her later.

My boyfriend ended up breaking my heart. The nurse got pregnant so he did the honorable thing and married her. The day he called to tell me I was in my bedroom with Karen after we had gone to the high school football game the night before. He and I had such a strong connection that I knew before the phone rang that he was calling me. I told Karen, "He is calling." The phone rang – that was the end. I never told my family what happened. I just stopped seeing him.

## *Almost Suicide - Attack*

I continued all my activities: working at the phone company, staying active at church, and helping with Youth for Christ. My life was spent reaching out to others, being there for them, listening to their problems, praying for them, I read my Bible, always went to church, and had many friends. In the midst of all that I felt very much alone, that no one was there for me when I was there for everyone else. I felt that my life was not worth anything. I began thinking that people could manage without me and that I did not need to be here. I planned my own suicide. I was going to do it in the car, hit a cement embankment at a speed that I knew would be fatal. I had it planned to the day and time.

The day before my planned suicide I was at the Youth for Christ Office and one of the pastors, Earl Bailey, called me into his office. I had not said anything to anyone. He asked me, "Karen, what is wrong?" I began weeping uncontrollably. I told him it was over for me. God sent him to me that day. He convinced me that my life was really just beginning and that God had a purpose for me. It was God's decision when my life should end. I learned that you can be serving God; helping people, doing a good job at work, have a loving family, and yet still feel alone, not satisfied personally, think you are nothing. Satan wants to gain our minds, our thinking. If he can make us think we are nothing we begin to believe it no matter how much good we are doing or what influence we are having.

As months passed, my thinking changed, my closeness to God grew. I became very content in what I was doing, that I was following what God wanted for my life. I thanked God for Earl and his wife Judy. They followed God's direction in their lives and moved to Indiana to minister there.

My cousin called and asked if I would stay with her young son when she had her second child. I thought it was a good time to get away. She went to the hospital and her second son was born. I was with her son at their home several days until she came home from the hospital. One night her husband came in drunk, celebrating the birth of their son. I was on the couch watching TV. He walked to me, picked me up and carried me to the bedroom. He attacked me sexually. He said he knew I had broken up with my boyfriend so he thought I would be willing until I told him that I was still a virgin. The next day he came and apologized again and again. I never told my cousin. I felt like it was somehow my fault, and that

I was not fit for anyone after that. Earl and Judy were nearby so I went and talked with them. They helped me through the situation. For some time after that I felt that my cousin's husband had some sort of hold on me. I carried the ordeal buried within me for about 20 years. As I counseled other people to deal with things in their lives, trust God, put the past in the past and move ahead with God's purpose, I dealt with my own past. God is good. I knew immediately that God had forgiven the situation but I did not forgive myself until 20 years later. I speak from personal experience that it is much better to deal with whatever comes in life immediately, forgive, seek forgiveness, and get back on track with God's purpose in life.

Don't dwell on the mistakes, the past, or the disappointments. Praise God anyhow.

# CHAPTER 4: JAMAICA

## *The Call – Lord Take My Hand*

We had a guest at Youth for Christ (Jim Lancaster) from Florida. He told us about a trip he had taken to Jamaica and the great desire there for the gospel. Jim was planning to take a group of young people the next summer to sing and minister for a week or so in Jamaica. My heart was touched and burdened for those people in Jamaica instantly. I went to Jim at the close of the meeting that night and told him I felt that I should go on the trip. He took my information and said he would contact me when the dates were set.

We were selecting vacations at the phone company. I was still very new there and knew I could not get vacation in July, plus I still had not received the exact dates for the trip. I ended up with January vacation. I put up a note and asked if anyone with a July vacation would consider trading. (Now what are the chances of that?) I prayed that if God really wanted me to go that He would work it out.

One lady came to me and said that she would trade, she thought she needed to get things done at home and would like an early vacation. I still did not have the dates. I told her I would let her know as soon as I got the dates. My January vacation was approaching and I had to let her know. I decided I would trade with her and pray that something worked out. When I got the dates they were for the very week that she traded me. God is good. I knew God must have something special for me on this trip. I went expecting my life to change – especially after God had orchestrated my being able to go.

Time came for the trip. I met the rest of the group at the airport in Miami. We flew from there to Jamaica. I cannot explain the emotions, feelings I had as we landed in Jamaica. Something was so stirring within me. I immediately loved the country and felt such a love for the people. We stayed several days at The Caribbean Christian Centre for the Deaf in Knockpatrick, Jamaica. We would go from there in the evenings to churches in the community. People would walk great distances to the churches. They were so hungry for the gospel that they would fill the church, and then fill the yards outside the church to hear us sing and the preaching.

Jim's wife, Irma, would sing 2 particular songs in the services: "_Precious Lord Take My Hand_" and "_Known Only to Him are the Great Hidden Secrets_". Every time she would sing I would feel God pulling me, taking my hand, and leading me to great things that only He knew were coming for me.

There were a few older students at the school who remained to cook and care for our group. School was out for the summer. One boy named Alden (8 years old) was still there awaiting someone to pick him up. He lived out in the bush. Alden had a wonderful smile and loved the attention from all of us. He taught us the Sign alphabet and some other signs. We were told that he had not yet accepted Christ as Savior because he did not know enough, did not understand.

Every morning at the deaf school we would meet on the veranda and have a time of worship, testimonies, and preaching from one of the pastors. It was our last morning there. Alden's mother had arrived to pick him up. She joined us on the veranda. After singing we began sharing how God was moving in many of our lives as a result of this journey. No one actually preached that morning. As we were closing in prayer Alden's mother stood up and said, "I want Jesus." My heart broke for Alden as I thought how little was said that morning but yet it was enough for his mother to realize that she needed Jesus. Yet Alden still did not know enough to choose Jesus.

We left for Kingston. Alden and his mother rode part way with us as we were going in the direction they were traveling. When we stopped the bus and they departed I began crying, thinking that I needed to do something to help Alden understand.

From there we went on to Kingston. In that last service, that last night in Kingston, again Irma got up and she was singing those songs

"_Known Only to Him are the Great Hidden Secrets_" and "_Precious Lord Take My Hand_". And now, I felt God really taking my hand leading me back there, to work with these deaf people, to teach them about Jesus, to learn Sign Language, and to be able to communicate.

As they closed the service that night I went to the director of the deaf school and I said to him, "Paul, if you have a job for me I will stay here now".  And he said to me, "You know, I've been watching you this week", and he said, "I just feel God is leading you to come here and work". And I agreed. I said, "Yes, I believe so too". And he told me, "What you need to do is go back and talk to your church, talk to your home churches", and he told me what I would need to have for financial support. He would stay in touch and we would work this out. He felt God would orchestrate for me to get back there as quickly as possible.

Well, that was in July, and in the month of September I returned after visiting several churches, my own home church, and some others that I had affiliation with. I went back to the church in Pennsylvania. I went to some other churches in the Ohio area and also in Florida. I shared with them my heart, what God has done, how I felt God was leading me to go to Jamaica to work with the deaf people there. I picked up a Sign Language book and began to study. I learned enough signs so that as I went to these churches, I could sing a song and sign it in Sign Language. Needless to say that the song I chose was "_Precious Lord Take My Hand_".

I just believed, trusted God, and went back and told the phone company I was leaving. They all thought I was crazy. They said, "Are you going to leave a job with security that will take you through your entire life? You want to give all that up and go out there where you don't know what you are going to have or if you are going to have enough money?" Some of the ladies that I worked with thought that was really crazy and I left knowing that I had left a tremendous testimony with them, the fact that I was willing to follow God, to give up all my security, everything that I had there, give up my apartment, give up everything I was doing, to follow what God was leading me to do.

## The Mission Field

In September when I returned to Jamaica, I went through Florida again and spent a few days with the Lancasters and Gonzales in Tampa, Florida. I visited their churches and had my first visit to Busch Gardens. They treated me. But I was anxious and so excited to get to the Mission field.

On my arrival, touchdown in Jamaica, I never forgot the feelings that I had as I arrived, that this is my place, this is what God has prepared me for. When I arrived they picked me up in a school van. On the journey to the deaf school I realized, I was there to stay. I had one main prayer when I came in and that was: "Dear God, please don't let there be any bugs in my bed". I knew that there were lots of bugs, lots of strange creatures that I wasn't used to coming from up north, but I said just: "don't let there be any in my bed".

I slept on a small (about half inch) mattress thrown over these spring-like things on this little frame. And I was put in the girl's dorm, doing all the motherly things, kind of being a dorm-mom. As well as learning the language and eventually helping-out in the class room teaching, I was working with them there. I also taught them some music.

I had no college preparation other than my year in nursing school and I had some emergency medical training. I had my high-school training. I had no other college or anything like that. I had a lot of training and preparation through the church. But God assured me that I knew what I needed to know to go, to be there.

And after that time when I had stood up in the service at age 15 and said, "Here am I Lord, send me" I waited five years before God called me and moved me to a specific place. I felt like, what's happening, during those years. I had given myself to God but he didn't take me, he didn't use me. What I realized, though, was that he had been planning and preparing and doing every little thing. All the things that had happened to me all the things that I was involved in, were all things preparing me and teaching me for the events to follow and the things God had me to do.

Like David's preparation while protecting sheep. I often relate things in my own life to that of David's.

All the students were back to school when I got there. School had started back up and all the students where there now, not just those that we had met on the trip. They started by giving me my name sign. We started getting aquatinted.

I met Miss Eunice who was the cook, the head person there in the kitchen. Throughout my time in Jamaica she took over as mom to me. She said, "I would want somebody to look after my daughter if they went to their country, I will do that for you." She would cook for me. And I remember the first time she served me a fish that looked like it hadn't been cooked. It had the head on and everything. But I thanked her and gracefully I peeled back the skin and ate the fish which was cooked and prepared well. It just didn't look like it was.

I learned to eat different foods, and enjoy all the things that I learned of the Jamaican culture, the people. I was anxious to learn more about them. Most of all I was anxious to learn the language of signs so that I could communicate with my new deaf friends and students.

I arrived in September, by late October I had learned enough signs that I would now begin to interpret some in the church service. We would take all the students by bus into one of the churches in Mandeville for evening or special services. Sunday mornings we often had our own services at the deaf school.

## *Teach - Learn - Preach*

One day after I had been there a few months, a call came that the school matron, who was the only one who taught classes there at the school, had an illness or a death or something in her family, and she had to leave. So they came to me and they said, "Karen, you take her classes". I began to panic as I thought, "How can I do that? I don't know enough signs to teach classes". But I thought, "Well, O.K.! If they want me to do this, I'll do this." I just trusted that God who called me there would prepare me for all he called me to do.

I would walk into the classroom and I would sign what I knew and finger-spell any words that I did not know. When I finger-spelled the word, they would give me the sign. They were teaching me signs and I would teach them subject matter. We would do science, math and different subjects.

I began to realize that they had very little concept of time. They said school started at such and such time but it started whenever the matron got ready to start, if it was that time or an hour later or two hours later. We were also located on a farm and raised our own crops, some chickens, some cattle. The students all worked on the farm as well as attended classes. So some days they would have classes and some days they wouldn't. It was just very un-organized, but yet quite an outreach.

They didn't have much television in Jamaica. Television came on in Jamaica about five o'clock, in the evening and went off the air about eleven o'clock. They had old shows from the U.S., and I think some news. That was how I learned about Kent State and some other events that happened during those years, through the TV broadcasts we did see there. I sent newsletters home and continued to learn the language.

We learned also that as we taught, preached, and had church services for the deaf, we didn't give alter calls/invitations very often. The deaf were so willing to please, that if there was something they thought you wanted them to do, they would do it just to please you. So, we would prepare the lessons and teach the things we thought God would have us to teach them but we would not give them the literal invitation at the close of the service. As I think back, and I look over that, I realized that's what happened to me in the Lutheran church. They had taught me the lessons, they had taught me the songs, but they didn't give me the invitation. Yet they had prepared me for the moment when the invitation was given to accept Christ as my personal Savior.

There were several times after we would have one of our lessons on a Sunday morning, or after we had been to one of the Church services in town, that one or two, sometimes a whole group of students, would come and say "I want Jesus". I will never forget the day that Alden was one of those students that came and said, "I want Jesus."

I knew in my heart that my original goal, my main purpose for going there, was being accomplished. I was to see Alden and many, many of the other students saved and come to know Jesus Christ as their personal Lord and Savior.

Coming from the states it may have seemed our buildings, methods, and our equipment was of back-woods or poor quality at the school. Things were about 50 years behind the times according to the way things were at home. It was still better than any of them would get out in the bush of Jamaica. Many of them had no opportunity to attend any school in Jamaica. And even the public schools in Jamaica were way behind what I was accustomed to in the states. The only better schools were the private, foreign operated schools.

God really impressed on me the fact that it needed to be upgraded and made better. So, I took it upon myself to develop a curriculum. (Not according to their ages, because they came to the school at various ages). We had one man 32 years old, a deaf man, who came to the school and had no sign background, no communication skills, and no education. He had to start at the very beginning. He knew nothing about math or any kind of subject matter, so he was actually in the beginning class.

I realized we had to set up the classes not according to their age group but according to their background and knowledge. I tried to group them accordingly. I remember the day he was so proud to recite his first Bible verse *"Jesus holler."* He was so excited that he got the wrong sign. He meant, *"Jesus wept."*

The matron had come back and we had another lady coming to begin teaching. We also had another missionary couple come to join us on staff who did not know signs. I started teaching Sign Language to them. There were three or four of them, that next summer, after I had arrived. I taught them Sign Language and communication skills.

I was so eager to learn that I picked up any books I could get. There was a lady who came to visit us that was versed in Total Communication skills. She taught me and I passed that on to the other teachers and people who were there to work in the deaf school

# LIFESONG - MY SYMPHONY

and learning about the deaf, even some of those ladies who worked in the kitchen. I was teaching them Sign Language and methods of teaching and all sorts of things I had watched my teachers do in the United States. I tried to teach these teachers how to do it. So I developed a school curriculum for each of the levels. I developed training methods for the teachers. All this was done within the first year I was there. God just lead me, gave me ideas. I continued to learn the language. I felt like it was a blessing from God that he gave me the language, but I was not only eager to learn it, but I felt like it wasn't something that I just sat down and studied. I felt that God gave it to me because he knew I needed it and he was ready for me to use it.

Me? Preach? A day came that the director of the school was to go to a group of young men preparing for the ministry. He realized he had something else that day at the same time. He asked me if I would go as a representative from the Deaf School. He told me to just do what they had him scheduled to do. I got there and was introduced to the leaders. They gave me a program. I saw Lester's name for invocation. *I can handle that.* They got further into the program and it came to message. I had not looked far enough on the program. Lester's name was there also and they were introducing me to bring the message. I breathed a quick prayer. *Help me Jesus!* I just began to share with them my testimony and scriptures that I had been reading in recent devotions, my scripture verse *Joshua 1:9.*

I encouraged them to be strong, trust God, and go do what God was preparing them to do. God showed me as they came to me after the service and told me how the words I shared had spoken into their lives that He can use us in ways and in times we feel we are not adequate to speak His word. When *He speaks* through a willing vessel – *It happens*.

## *Piano*

I taught piano to some of our deaf students. They loved it. They would walk into the room with hard wood floors and a big upright piano and say "Oh! She is playing this song or that song" and people wondered how they would know that, because they didn't hear it.

They would feel it; they would feel the vibration through the wooden floor. They came up and put their hands on the piano, or they would come up and they would say, "Play this particular song", because they liked the way it felt. They would be able to know by the feeling, what they were feeling through the woodwork, what I was playing. So that taught me that physical feeling is so important. God had shown me as he worked all these things musically that the senses reach us deeply and provide so much for feelings and emotions. How the things that are physically felt reach us and teach us. When I started teaching speech and voice lessons I used the same kind of concept. I taught to create the sounds and vocal expressions in relationship to the particular feelings in the body. You know when you get it right by how it feels. I realized that the deaf were enjoying this, and liking this.

## *Missionary Friends*

While I was there I met other missionaries that lived in a place not far from us, Maypen. I would visit them occasionally. Some glorious things happened there so far as my outreach musically.

One time the missionaries in Maypen asked me to come because they were having a mission group coming in from the States and they wanted me to meet these people. Mack Evans was with them on that trip. They were from Landmark Baptist Temple. Mack Evans had driven the bus for them from the Church to the airport in Miami and had not planned to come along with them on the trip. They convinced him that God had something for him in Jamaica. And, in case you don't know, Mack was involved with gospel quartets and I had heard him before. He was another one that as he began to sing, there in Jamaica, God really touched my heart and blessed me through his music and through his ministry.

I saw God really touch and work in his life through those days they visited the mission field. Also he was the first person, the first musician that I had the opportunity to interpret for, and that was such a blessing to me. God's special touch often reaches me through music and Sign Language Interpreting: **WORSHIP**.

Mack ended up in ministry with Jerry Farwell and the gospel trio. It was my special blessing to meet Mack, to be able to interpret for him and later he came to the church in Canton after I had returned from the mission field. I spoke with him and reminisced how he was the first musician I had interpreted for and the days we shared in God's presence and blessing in Jamaica.

Through the years his music has been very special to me. I know his singing "<u>Hallelujah, Oh What a Savior</u>" in Jamaica was used by God to prick my heart. I also remember while the group was there and visiting from Landmark we took them out to the country and we held some street meetings. We watched the people of Jamaica respond so hungrily to the Gospel. It was just a very thrilling, awesome experience for me.

## *Yield To Temptation*

One of the men that I worked for there at the school was very instrumental in the operation of the school. He and I worked very closely, too closely. I found that we spent many, many, many hours a day working in very close quarters and I learned to love and appreciate him for his testimony, for the churches he established all across the island of Jamaica, and for his ministry. He had shared his testimony with us when our group had first visited there. I was just impressed by how God had moved him and worked in his life. He seemed to become interested in me in the same way. He respected my testimony and God's leading in my life to bring me to Jamaica.

So we learned a love and respect for each other's walk with God and ministry and what God had done for us. As we worked so closely, so many hours a day, in such close quarters, he began to share with me things from his family, from his home life, and some things I wasn't sure he should have been sharing. There was no one else there. We had to get the work done and we became too close. He began to really rely on me for things at the school.

One day as we were traveling to Kingston he reached over and put his hand on mine and I went to pull it away, he held it and made a comment about how I had shared with him what happened with my boyfriend before I came to Jamaica. And he expressed a sorrow at the fact that I had lost someone that I had cared about. He told me that God would have someone for me. He began to show an interest in me. And as we spent time together we grew closer and closer. We ended up having a relationship we should not have had and a type of relationship we should not have shared.

It's the same thing I have seen over and over and over again throughout the years of my life. One thing that I had felt was, as a result of losing my boyfriend and of course the incident with the relative, I felt that "No one will ever love me", "No one will ever care about me." I thought, "He knew all of that and yet he thought I was worthwhile". He thought I was somebody that could be meaningful to someone in a relationship. I think because of that Satan convinced me that I could be O.K. with him and have a safe relationship with him because, after all, he loved God and I loved God.

Things happened that shouldn't have, and we became involved in a sexual relationship. I immediately become pregnant as I suspected I would if I gave in to sexual temptation and said I would as a young teen, I learned that what you say is what you get. I dealt with the fact that I had become pregnant.

Once again, I had a secret that I held deep within me. I did not tell anyone. I didn't even tell him for a long time. Finally, I did confess to him and I didn't go to a doctor until I was over 6 months pregnant. I continued everything I was doing there at the school. Some days when I would go in for the morning devotions and to teach classes I would almost pass out. I would black out to where I would see nothing but black and I would still walk down the hall as though I knew exactly what I was doing. I tried to hide it all the way and finally I was 6 1/2 months pregnant. I had an opportunity to go home for Christmas and I felt like I should go, get away, go for the holidays.

I tried to hide the pregnancy. I hid it like I was just gaining weight; you know, like good Jamaican food, lots of fried things, so I hid it that way. I wore bigger clothes and thought no one really knew what was going on. My family always thought of me as fat anyway. So I decided to go there for the holidays. I went home and visited with my family. They kept commenting, "Oh my goodness! You gained so much weight!" and "Look how fat she is." The thing that really got me about that was from the time I was young, in school; my parents always were on me about being chunky and too overweight. Through high school I felt the same way.

I went back and looked at pictures, I realized I wasn't as big as I thought I was, but I always had the feeling that I was fat. After all, I had always been told I was. Of course, at that time, when I went home it was legitimate. I knew I was. I also knew it was temporary but it really bothered me that they commented so much about my weight, in fact it didn't seem to raise any suspicions that I might be pregnant. The flight home made my feet and legs swell terribly, but again, I tried to hide it. I covered it all.

Even with my good buddy, I saw Karen and her family, and I didn't even tell her. I guess I was 6 ½ months pregnant and I just did not tell her what had happened. But during that trip home I thought, "What am I going to do as far as having this baby? If I have it in the country of Jamaica and they realize that the father is from there, when I return back to the U.S.A., there will be a problem with nationalities. Being a single parent, I may not be allowed to take the child out of the country?" And I also considered, "Should I have this child? Should I adopt this child? Should I have an abortion?" All of those things crossed my mind earlier and all of those things I had discussed with the father at the time. What are the possibilities? He encouraged me, at one point, to have an abortion but it wasn't long until I knew I couldn't do that, and he realized that I could not.

We decided that I would contact someone in the States. I would go to the States to have my child. Then I would decide to put my child up for adoption or whatever from that point. I didn't know who to call and the only person I knew I could reach out to would be my cousin, the one who had the baby and I had gone and stayed in their home. So I called her and asked her if I could come to her home. I knew that her husband would be there and even with all that had happened before, I didn't know where else to go.

She agreed and said I could come there. So very soon after returning from the Christmas holidays I went to my cousin's. There were a lot of things I dealt with. Before I left Jamaica there was a confrontation with my child's father's wife who confronted me as though she knew everything. I felt like the father had betrayed me by telling his wife when we had agreed to spare her and their children. I found out later that she was just guessing. It was a lot to take, particularly after holding everything inside, not telling anyone.

I learned later that Karen's mother had asked her, "Could Karen be pregnant?" Karen told her, "Oh no! She just gained weight being down there, you know!" So even Karen didn't know or suspect. I didn't share it with her.

After I arrived at my cousin's I met some friends of my cousin that lived across the street from her that took in foster children. Immediately they told me that they might be interested in adopting my baby. I thought that might be a good plan. I knew she would have a decent home, and things could work that way. Maybe that was why God made a way for me to be there.

I felt I needed to go and complete the job that God had me start in Jamaica. Even if I only stayed the rest of the two year term that was originally agreed on I had to go and finish that. I had set up the curriculum and the teachers and all within that first year and I wanted to see all of those things completed.

I went to my cousin, my baby was born, and the hospital stay was horrible. I went to the hospital, and this was in the days that unwed mothers weren't accepted. Unwed mothers should never be rejected as human beings or as a person needing care and treatment. But I went into the hospital, and because I was an unwed mother, I was not allowed to have any visitors except immediate family. I had no immediate family there. My cousin was the closest, so they did give her permission to visit me. But she was the only one allowed to visit me.

After my daughter was born, after a couple of days they would not bring her to me. I realized they were not bringing her for her feedings or visits. That was also in the days before the child was in the room with the mother and all of those nice conveniences there are today. So I started asking "Why aren't you bringing my baby to me?" and I began to get scared, I thought they had taken my child from me, I didn't know what they were doing. I just felt like something had gone wrong, that they were taking my child from me and not telling me.

What they didn't tell me was that the reason they were not bringing her in was because I had a fever. So I went through a couple of days not seeing my baby, not knowing what was happening. Finally I was released from the hospital and went back to my cousin's with the baby.

Her husband confronted me and accused me of being so righteous and holy before. I had told him I hadn't had sex, and didn't want to. Here I come and I show-up there pregnant. I felt like I had ruined my testimony there, even though the situation had happened there before. I still tried to be forgiving and understanding and be a witness to my cousin and her family. So I did feel in some ways that I let them down. I also felt that I let down my church, my family, and most importantly God. I felt I let Him down by yielding to the temptation and committing the sin.

However I realized and knew that the child was not the sin. It was the sex that was the sin but the child was a blessing. She was a beauty. She was a joy. She was a delight, a gift from God. My good buddy, Karen, was the one that said to me, then and many times since that, "God knew what he was doing when he gave you Leslie". Because she knew that with all the things that I had gone through, thought about, and faced that I might have reverted back to the thought of suicide or whatever. But because of having a child now, someone that needed me, she knew that I would no longer consider suicide.

After I had gone to my cousin, before Leslie was born, I knew I needed to call my parents and tell them what was going on. I felt that they would be either totally accepting of the fact, not approving what I had done, but accepting the fact that this had happened and they will love me and go on, or they would ask me to just totally leave the family. I felt that it would be one or the other, no middle of the road. I wasn't sure how that would go. I called my parents and told them over the telephone that I was pregnant, and I was expecting in March. It just so happened that my father was going on a business meeting, flying to Indiana the next week-end. So my cousin and I arranged to see him and meet with him. We picked him up at the airport, visited with him and he stayed at my cousin's a couple of days.

We took him back to the airport and as we were leaving the airport, I had my first labor pain. We went home and a huge snow storm came in. I was taken to the hospital in the early morning, sliding on the frozen roads.

I was very thankful that my parents did react the way they did: were forgiving, understanding.

There was also a time before I returned to Jamaica, that my father came and took Leslie and I back to Ohio. My family met her, and Mary and Ralph (like my second mom & dad) met Leslie. My mother was forgiving but she was also embarrassed. She did not want me to take my baby to public places, where she worked, etc.

Then came the time for the return, I just still felt that I needed to go back and finish that term in Jamaica that I had started. Meanwhile, the father had called me and told me that his sister would allow Leslie to stay with her which meant that I could leave her in Montigo Bay. I knew his sister and trusted her very much. On weekends I would leave the school and go spend it with Leslie. I knew it would not be proper, of course, to have Leslie at the school. They still did not know that I had gone to have a child.

I took her, went back to Jamaica, I will never forget the day I had to leave her in Montigo Bay. And the weeks seemed so very long, very tedious, and then I would go on Fridays as soon as we finished things at school. I would go, spend the weekend, and return Sunday evenings. They were precious times that I had with her. I also had hired a nursemaid to take care of her during the week. I got someone to totally take care of her, paid her for around the clock child care. That lasted for the few months that I was there, in Jamaica.

There was someone on the board that became aware I had a child. Leslie's father's wife had told them. She made known to them what had taken place. They called me in and they talked. We agreed that I would leave. The board was aware that I did have a child, so of course there was no offer to renew my stay.

When Leslie was six months old and my two-year term was up, I left and returned to Ohio. I went back to my parents.

*Psalm 100 -*
*Make a joyful noise unto the Lord, all ye lands.*
*Serve the Lord with gladness; come before his presence with singing. Know ye that the lord, he is God; it is he that hath made us, and not we ourselves; we are his people, and the sheep of his pasture. Enter into his gates with thanksgiving, and into His courts with praise; be thankful unto him, and bless his name. For the Lord is good; His mercy is everlasting, and His truth endureth to all generations.*

# CHAPTER 5: OHIO THE RETURN

## *Admitting Failure*

I checked at the phone company to see if there were any possibilities of getting back on there. There were no openings at that time but they took my application and said they would hold it.

I went to church. I did not take Leslie the first Sunday I was back. I went to see the pastor from my church. It was the younger pastor that I spoke with and told him what had happened. He asked if I would please come before the deacons of the church and just let them know, be aware, talk to them a little bit, tell them what had happened. So that as I showed up in church with a baby, people would have questions and they would have answers for the people, and they would be able to help me, to keep me from embarrassment and things.

I did and it was one of the hardest things in my life, to have to stand before those men and tell them, admitting that I had failed because I felt like I went out representing God, representing them, my church as I went to the mission field. I felt like I had to stand up and let them know that I had failed and because of my background, failure was just not something that was acceptable.

Flunking out of the nursing school was also a very traumatic time. I knew that failure was not something that was accepted by my family. Even though I had good grades in school I always knew if I didn't get the "A" or at least the "B", that I'd be in trouble, that I had to really strive for that. I had learned early to strive for perfection. And I became that way in everything I did. I wanted to do things right, the best they could be done. I was that way in my music; I was that way in my work, and that way in raising my daughter, and that way in going to school, later on, down the road. And I thought everything I did had to be right. And each time I would have some sort of failure I felt like it had to be even more perfect the next time around.

I started to work at the church. They needed someone to help in the office, church secretarial work. I did that knowing that I was hoping at some point to get back to the telephone company. But until that happened, I would work at the church office.

During that time the people at church were very loving, very caring. My neighbors, my friends, much to my surprise, really everyone who had loved and supported me before I left, still seemed to love and care for me and love my child. There were no bad feelings against me or things that I had done.

I began a new life there or a life again. I became involved very quickly, again, with the things at the church. I started a new singing group there; I was also working with the youth, singing in the choir again and playing instruments. So in a very short time I was very involved again with my church. So I appreciated my church for being not one of those who, because you had a visible reflection of some sin in your life, didn't allow you to take part or be active in the church, as some did in that day and time.

## *Offerings*

One thing that was introduced to my church shortly after my return from Jamaica was something called Faith Promise Offerings. What that was: you gave your regular tithes and offerings and then God will impress upon you an amount that you were to give for a year period of time, either weekly, or one lump sum, or monthly, or however, just whatever you felt God was telling you to do. But the catch was: you didn't give it until God supplied that for you in some extra way that wasn't something that you already had. It was something that you'd believe God would supply to you.

I asked God to give me a figure, just something he would have me to give, something to believe him for, trust him for. And I knew God had forgiven me for all the ways that I felt I had let him down. He had restored me, lifted me back up. I thought, "I am going to take a step of faith and believe God to give me an amount". And he did. He laid a certain amount on my heart and I began praying about it. I said "OK God! This is going to be something you are going to have to do, if I am going to be able to give this money, you are going to have to provide that for me in some way."

The Sunday came that we were going to take this pledge, this faith promise offering. Some were giving amounts that day; others said how much they intended to give and whether it would be weekly, monthly, annually, or whatever. I put my amount on the paper and turned it in.

The next day, in the church office, part of my duties were to count that offering, to add the faith promise for the entire church for the year and see what it was going to be. I was sitting in the office doing that when the telephone rang and it was the telephone company, telling me that now they have some openings and some positions available if I was interested in coming back to work. But the most fantastic thing was that the difference in the two salaries: what I was making as the church secretary and what I will be making at the telephone company was the amount of my faith promise.

I knew that God was faithful and he had provided as he said he would. I started giving that on a weekly basis as I went back to the other job. God has never failed me. That was the first year and each year after that for several years we took faith promise offerings and I just followed God. Each time he always provided, made the way and he blessed me in ways that I didn't expect or imagine.

I went back to the telephone company.

## *He Touched Me – While Serving*

I had a singing group: some high-school kids. We were known as the "Bread O' Life" and we traveled around the area, as well as singing in our own church. God really blessed us through the ministry of "Bread O' Life". We just felt God leading us in the songs that we sang and God gave us a heart for people and a heart for ministering.

There was one Sunday that I did not feel well, for a few days I had a cold/flu, something. On this particular Sunday I got up and I had this horrible, horrible headache and fever. Our group was scheduled to sing at a church that afternoon, out of town. It was a very special program that had been planned for a long time. There was no one else that could lead the group, or play the piano for them. They could have done some of the songs but not everything. I was the only one that played some of the songs. So I dragged myself out of bed, got dressed and went to the concert. I was also wringing wet from perspiration due to the fever. So I prayed and trusted God to get us through that concert.

The concert began, God blessed over and over again through so many of the songs, we could tell by how the people were reacting that they were being reached wonderfully through the music and through the testimonies that we were sharing. I sang, I played and I led the group. The song "*He Touched Me*" became a reality to me as I played it. I knew I was only making it through because of His touch. I made it, but nearly collapsed. We realized that my fever was probably 105* that day. After near collapse, I got home and I felt like my head was just going to blow off - explode. I had such tremendous pressure in my head and I didn't get out of bed for 3 days. Finally I was lying there in my bed very sick.

I remember lying there and sensing that spirits were battling over me. I felt like evil spirits were trying to just come and take me away. I finally just sat up in the bed and said "You might as well get away from me because I am God's and as long as He lets me live I am going to live for God. If you are trying to take me or influence me, you might as well getaway, get behind me Satan." Then a peace came, my fever broke, I recovered, and a couple of weeks later I developed these white chalky looking things on the back of my throat. I went to the doctor.

Now, the weekend that I had been sick, those couple of days, I had called the doctor's office but he was of town. I thought it was a cold, a winter cold, flu, or something. So I didn't bother after I began feeling better. After the doctor took a look at my throat he took some cultures, and after the tests came back he told me I had mononucleosis. "Do you know you could have died?" he said. "Your fever must have been tremendously high" and I said, "Yes".

I knew that I was dying. I felt like I was dying. I realized that I was on the point of death and God had spared me, and that he must have another purpose for me, a reason for me to go on in life. I just came out with a new vision for God feeling that God had something more wonderful ahead for the lives of Leslie and me.

## *The Call – Baptist Bible College*

I went on working at the telephone company and doing many things at the church. Out of my group there were three of the kids that were graduating that year and they were going to Baptist Bible College in Springfield, Missouri. There was one young man and woman in the group that got married as they were seniors in high school because she had become pregnant. They called me and talked to me and I counseled with them. Because of the things that I had gone through and being a single parent, I was able to reach out to her especially in some ways that I know others could not have. So I thanked God for that opportunity to be able to share. And I asked God to give me more of those situations that I could share from the things that I have been through, to possibly help others to know that they can make it through things in life, that God can bless them and turn things around for his honor and his glory.

I was used by them as a reference when they were applying to the college. That young man and another young man in my group were going to Bible Baptist College. When you are a reference for someone, they usually will send you a form to fill out, to give references about this person or your recommendation or non-recommendations. With only one of their referral papers was enclosed an application and I thought this was strange, why were they sending me an application to Baptist Bible College when, you know, I was sending them this reference. An application only came with one, not both of the referrals.

I thought about that, started praying about it. What was God saying to me, "I want you to go there"? I always had this desire to go back to school, and I felt that one day I would, and I thought, "O.K., I would love to do this!" but being an unwed mother I didn't know if they would even consider me. And I thought, "Well, I got this application for a reason and God must want me to do something with this". So I filled it out and sent it in.

Also I stepped out in faith and went to them at work, at the telephone company, and put in a transfer request for Springfield, Missouri. I thought, "Well, if the transfer goes through, maybe that will be a sign that I am supposed to go there and go to bible school."

Then I started another one of those waiting periods, I didn't get the application back. I didn't hear back from my transfer. Then finally I did get the application back, low and behold, I was accepted. Then this thing came in at work and they said, "We have good news, and we have bad news." I said, "Well, O.K what is it?" and they said: "Your application for transfer came back rejected."I thought, "O.K.! Maybe that's God telling me I am not supposed to go there" "However" they said, "the reason given was because you didn't have enough continuous service with the company. The union saw it and read it before we even gave it to you.

They filed a grievance before it ever came to you. So it has now come back approved. The union went to them and said that you had two years nine months of continuous service with us before you left for Jamaica and you are now back six months and that should count as time of continuous service, and that your work record is good."

So once again God orchestrated in a very wonderful way a move for me that I knew was something he was leading me into. That summer Leslie and I packed up and made preparations to go to Missouri. I loaded the car (I had gotten a Buick Skylark '69). There was room for me and her car seat in front, the rest was jam packed, full with a luggage rack on top and was full of almost everything I owned. I loaded up and headed for Springfield, Missouri.

# CHAPTER 6: MISSOURI

## *Getting Settled*

All I knew was that next Monday I would start the job in Springfield. I left, I think it was somewhere in the middle of the week; Wednesday or Thursday, something like that, no later than a Friday. It took us two days, I believe, we stopped one night and pulled into Springfield, Missouri, actually on a Saturday morning. I had no place to live. I knew I had been accepted at the Bible school. So I knew I could go there.

I knew I had a place to work, but I had no place to live, I had no baby sitter. I just went there believing that God was going to work all these things out. I had learned from the Jamaica experience, that when God says go, when you feel that God is leading you into something, if you just trust him and follow him and believe him, he makes a way. I drove into town, bought a newspaper, we sat at McDonald's eating breakfast and I looked in the newspaper for apartments that were available. I started making some phone calls, made arrangements to meet with a lady in a house. She had an apartment that was in this house and I had looked at a couple of places but this one in particular just, I don't know, just struck me in the paper. I met her that day and decided that will be the place for us.

She had two apartments downstairs and two upstairs, each had its own private key into the apartment. We all went into the front door and then went from the hallway into our own apartment. It was very small. I had one tiny bathroom, a very small little kitchen corner, barely room enough for this little 2x2 table. It had a stove, a refrigerator and that was it. You could almost turn around in there. And it had a living room and a bedroom under a staircase. So we moved in there - it was furnished. I did not have any furniture at that time, so we needed to have a place that was furnished.

The people next door, in the other apartment downstairs, saw us coming in and they came out and introduced themselves.

# LIFESONG - MY SYMPHONY

The little lady, she said to just call her Granny, said this is my daughter and this is her son. Her son was a year older than Leslie, who was two at the time we moved. Granny said, "I baby sit for him all the time when my daughter works." Granny had a son who lived there as well.

So I met them all that day, and we were talking about the fact that I was coming here to go to Bible school and worked at the phone company. We talked about plans for Leslie and Granny said: "I am here all day anyway. I take care of Tommy and baby-sit for him. It will be good for him to have company. Why don't I just keep your daughter?" So that was the beginning, she did baby sit Leslie and she was just like "Granny". She was "Granny" to both of us. She took care of Leslie.

The day we moved in, everything was taken care of. We had a home and we had a baby-sitter. Monday I started the job and I also went that week to check about school. So it looked like everything was falling into place for what we were supposed to do there. That began a fifteen year stay in Springfield. A stay that I originally thought was going to be three years, long enough for me to get an Associate degree in music. Many things happened through those fifteen years. I will continue and share some of those experiences.

I just want you, the reader, to see and know how God can truly lead you if you will let him. When he tells you something, just follow it; take it as a directive as you feel it in your heart. You may not hear it in an audible voice. Other than that time as a child in the garden, when I thought somebody was calling my name, I never heard an audible voice directing me or instructing me. I never audibly heard: "Go to Springfield, Missouri" or go to "Knockpatrick, Jamaica". I just knew in my heart that was what God was telling me to do and knowing that, and believing that, I stepped out and trusted in faith and followed and ended up in the place where I know that God just truly wanted me to be.

One of the first things when I arrived in Springfield was to go to the President of the college and meet with him. I sat down with him and talked. I let him know that I was there, that I arrived and I had gotten an apartment. I knew the rules require that first and second year students live on campus, but I also figured, because of my situation, being an unwed mother, they would probably want me to live off campus, and after talking to him, that was the case, that was what they wanted. I lived off campus and worked at the phone company. I started work there, Monday after I arrived in town, on Saturday. I started visiting churches.

The day I went to work, I went in, signed in, registered my vehicle and they gave a card decal to put on my car. I went out on my lunch hour, to put the sticker on my car, my car which had been registered with security, they were supposedly aware of it, but my car had been towed. Of course I had an Ohio license plate and the little storage thing was still on the roof. My new Supervisor Virginia (who became my great friend) took me to retrieve my car after work. Yes – I had to pay the towing fee.

## *My Tribute*

As I started there at the Bible College, I began studying music. During my first semester the music department head was my piano instructor. That normally didn't happen with freshman students, but because the volume of students that year was high he had to take freshman students. So I studied piano with him one semester and after that he had me switch to Bub Everett, who was my teacher throughout the remaining years there at the college.

I began attending church at the South Side Baptist Church where Mr. Everett was the music director. I sang in the choir, directed the children's choir, and eventually worked with a youth choir. I played and sang in a ladies group, and played in the band at Church and at school. I played trombone after not playing it since high school. I enjoyed my studies very much. My first semester, under Mr. Everett, I got a "B" in piano which frustrated me very much. I still had the idea that I had to be a perfectionist and get the "A" as much as possible and do everything absolutely right. My goal was to be a four-pointer. When I got a "B" and not an "A" I went in and talked to Mr. Everett.

Two other of his students also got "B" and had the same feelings. I remember him explaining to us that an "A" in piano means that there is no room for improvement. We expressed our disagreement with him, considering the fact that we had completed our assignments for that semester.

Through the years I did get some "A"s from Mr. Everett, but the more I thought about it, Mr. Everett was probably right, that it should be very rare that an "A" is given in those types of studies, because there is always room for improvement, particularly in instrument or voice. However, I got over that and I learned so much there. The things that had been frustrating to me with the piano teacher in Ohio I began to understand. Once I knew what she was talking about, it all made sense and I learned very quickly. Time flew by as I studied music and Bible, worked full time, and I raised Leslie.

During the second year of school, we had to return home for my father's open heart surgery. I had trouble getting home in a snowstorm. (I need to write a book sometime about traveling frustrations, I can speak from experience). I remember praying and seeking God, and asking God to let my father live to see me graduate from college. He recuperated from the open heart surgery. We returned and I continued on with school. My father came to my graduation. He died a few years later of pancreatic cancer.

I remember an August trip home, seeing my father so thin and weak. I knew when I left from my visit home that I would probably not see my father alive again. He died the following November.

The semester when my father had his heart problem, I was in a class that was considered one of the most difficult, Bible History. I had the most difficult professor. Having to miss a week of class with him was very devastating. Consequently, I actually failed that class that semester and had to retake it. But even though in his class I failed, I learned so much more from him than I did in a lot of other classes. I did re-take it, and passed it. It was one of those required classes, and you had to pass in order to graduate from the Bible College.

By the time I reached my third year there, a four year program was developed for music. So at the end of the third year I graduated with an Associate degree in music and I stayed on for the four year program and double majored in piano performance and in music composition.

# LIFESONG - MY SYMPHONY

I remember my first jury, (a piano major had to come in and play a piece in front of music faculty for approval to move on to the next semester or for approval to perform in a recital.) and after I played it I went out, it was winter time, stormy, and I slipped and fell on the ice and hit my elbow, my funny bone. I was glad it happened after the jury instead of before but none the less I had done it. It hurt for a long time.

Also, during my time there several students had some frustrations with the head of the department. For some reason he gave us a hard time as far as scheduling recitals after we were approved to do them and we had to reschedule. He didn't like the way they were scheduled and who we were scheduled with because you gave junior recitals or freshman, sophomore recitals with other students. (Freshman - sophomore recitals, you play or sing one piece on a group recital or in a junior recital there were two people in recitals and he didn't like some of the combinations.) Anyway we had some frustrations dealing with that, but we got through it.

I came down to my senior year. Another girl and I were going to have our juries on the same day. For the senior recital you go before the music faculty and you play portions of the pieces you had prepared for your recital, and then they will approve it or disapprove it. If you are approved you are allowed to go ahead and schedule and give your recital. So she and I were going on the same day to be approved. She and I decided to meet together and prepare with prayer before going in for our jury.

We prayed together and I remember us praying very seriously. I always took prayer seriously. I always meant what I prayed and I didn't pray non-sealant. I prayed, "If I can serve you better Lord without my hands, you can have them." My friend said to me later that she couldn't believe I really prayed that prayer.

We went in; we were both approved, that day. That night, I was driving. We had a girl living with us, sharing the apartment expenses. I would often pick her up from work, and as we were returning to our house, a car ran a light, right in front of me, I slammed on the brakes, we collided with them and I grabbed the steering wheel and injured my wrists. No one else was injured.

# LIFESONG - MY SYMPHONY

I very quickly remembered my prayer, I began having all these sensations and feelings, my hands felt like they were swelling and there were a lot of sensations on my arm – like tingling, falling asleep. I had a battery of neurological tests; they felt that it was something that would take time to heal. I don't believe I ever returned to the same musical dexterity and technicality, the control, that I had before. But as I began to study and come back, it became very evident, very quickly that I was not going to be able to do my senior piano recital. Fortunately for me, I had taken a double major, so I was still able to graduate that year with the music composition degree, and for that degree I had to write an entire recital of music and have it performed, do a complete recital. That was a lot of fun. I really enjoyed the composing and the study, the writing of music.

I was thankful I had taken the double major because I could still graduate, finish my course. However, I still wanted the piano degree and I was unable at that time to get it. I always had in my mind the memory of surrendering my hands through "_Precious Lord take my Hand_" and prayer. I also was reminded that often what we say is what we get. God pays attention to what we say/pray.

We were in Springfield, Missouri, the home of Southwest Missouri State University and they had quite an extensive music program there. So I thought I might go and pick up a couple of education classes in music. I then had an Associate degree in music and Bible, and a Bachelor of Arts degree in music composition. I thought I would go take a couple of education classes, add to my education until I can complete my recital.

I went ahead and enrolled into Southwest Missouri State University, and I began studying piano there under Mr. Adler. He had played with some big bands and I enjoyed studying under him. As I was studying with him I was still studying with Mr. Everett. My hands would reach a certain point, certain dexterity as I was practicing the pieces and then all of a sudden, they would just give out again. Improvement came in stages. Then I would back-up and start again, and I would get a little bit further the next time. I kept doing that as I kept taking these other classes. For the State University education degree in music you had to do a recital.

It was not as extensive a recital as the piano performance recital would have been for the bachelor of music degree in piano performance.

Since the recital was the only requirement I was lacking for my piano performance degree, Baptist Bible College agreed that if I would recover enough to go complete a recital to meet the qualifications for the education degree at Southwest Missouri State University, they would grant me my piano performance degree as well.

At Baptist Bible College I taught and trained people that were going to be working in ministries across the country and around the world. I was on staff there and they used me as a supply teacher in music. After I graduated with the composition degree, I was a supply teacher for piano class. I also taught some of the music education classes; usually one or two classes per semester as well as piano lab and of course my Sign Language and interpreting class. At the same time I was studying at the State University.

So after 2 years Baptist Bible College scheduled me for a recital. We felt my hands had improved enough to get through it. They booked it as a faculty recital since I was part of the faculty. That meant that every music student was required to attend. That put a little extra pressure on me. I had not played publicly since the time of the accident; this was going to be the first public performance. I came back and I started to play through the recital and I got parts of it O.K. Then I started having some problems with memory. The recital had to be totally memorized. There were some of the pieces that I didn't do as well as I should have, and one piece I actually, totally lost memory in the middle. I finally found my way back and concluded it. What I played in the middle I am not quite sure.

I prayed that God would restore my hands that I could come back and play "_My Tribute_" – _To God Be the Glory_", a special arrangement I had prepared for the original recital. It was one song that I was able to at least play through at the recital. And I know that there were a couple of people who came to the recital from work who were very blessed and moved by that song. So, even though, in a way it seemed a total failure, to them, as outsiders, they didn't recognize the lack of technique and memory. The music students, and of course the music faculty were very aware of

# LIFESONG - MY SYMPHONY

the poor job that I had done. So, once again I had one of those failure experiences, and I was very devastated by it.

A few months later some of my musician friends and I went to a concert by Van Clyburn (My favorite of his is "*Summer of 42*"). Some of us music students met him back stage after the concert. He shared with us how he lost memory one time playing Chopin I believe. He told us he improvised and how his instructor was so impressed with what he played. Made me feel better although I know my improvisation was probably nothing like his.

Then, after time, I was approaching the recital at the State University. I really came to God in prayer and said: "Oh! God! I need your help!" I think part of it was just because I had this fear of my hands giving out in the middle, my memory giving out. I was really trusting God and He helped me through it. The recital went very well, and I was able to complete it. "*My Tribute*" was the best.

I was able to complete my degree at the Southwest Missouri State University. That recital gave me a Bachelor of Arts degree in Piano Performance, Bachelor of Arts degree in Piano Composition, after my Associate degree as well as now a Bachelor of Science in Education degree. I became certified K through 12.

After those experiences I had the desire to accompany, to play for the choir, things like I have done before. I never did like the solo work or being the featured pianist. I always felt like, that wasn't for me, that I was one to play for the group or play with an ensemble, play in the smaller bands, whatever. Through the years I was involved in many groups and activities vocally. I was in duets, the choirs, and the ensembles. Again I never felt that I was the one to be the soloist, which was not my forte.

That song, "*My Tribute*" has driven me from then on. I wanted my life, my testimony, to be To God be the Glory. Often when I did play a solo or a feature it would either be that song or something that expresses that feeling: to God be the glory. And I have learned to worship him and praise him through my music.

I spent about 15 years in Springfield and I think about 13 of those I was in school in some way or another. The first 4 years at Baptist Bible College were as a full time student as well as working full time. Then I started taking just a couple of classes at a time, working towards a "Bachelor of Science and Master of Science in Education" degree. So it took me several years to get through. I became known as a professional student.

I enjoyed my college life, I enjoyed the classes, I enjoyed my professors, I enjoyed the study, and God was very good to me. He kept putting me in the right places. I know that Baptist Bible College developed a four year music program *just for me*, and the Southwest Missouri State University developed a deaf education program *just for me*, might have been for somebody else too, but I know that they were there *just for me* and God had me there for those purposes.

## *The Deaf*

I continued on at the State University. Again God did a wonderful thing *just for me*. As I was finishing the education degree, they opened up a brand new program at the State University in Deaf Education and it was a Masters program. I went ahead and enrolled in the masters program and decided to go on and study Deaf Education.

I first completed enough courses to add a deaf education certification to my Bachelor of Science in Education degree. I now became, not only, certified music K through 12, but in Deaf Education as well. I went on to finish the classes for my masters. Again I had some problems with one professor while working on my Master of Science in Education. My master's thesis was on how to teach music to the Deaf and benefits of music classes for the Deaf students in the public school system.

I had many wonderful professors, people who were very knowledgeable and educated in the field with great backgrounds. I learned so much more to add to the practical experiences and knowledge that I had gained through the many years of working with the deaf from the time in Jamaica, the time in Churches, and working with Deaf people across the country.

I had interpreted in medical situations, in legal situations and on the job training situations. So many great experiences as well as in Church interpreting and teaching and training in Sign Language and interpreting. I was very involved in music and with the Deaf.

## *Raising Leslie*
### *- Signing Together*

After five or six years there in Springfield, my daughter was growing up. She started school and she ended up going to the elementary school that had the deaf students in the city. She started learning Sign Language with them at the school and then came home and because of my knowledge and background we did a lot of it together. Through the years there, even though she was a young child, she would go with me and she would help me teach my classes. From that point on as I was teaching classes in Church and in various places around the city, Leslie was with me. She became very proficient as well as a very good interpreter at a very young age (about 10). She not only had it in school but she became great friends with one of the deaf girls in school. She became very fluent and it was something that we would do together.

### *- Dance & Pageants*

Let me take you back to some of the other happenings before leaving Springfield:

Through those years my daughter was growing up and, of course, started school. Leslie was now in high school, she was a senior, and had been studying dance and modeling at Sunshine Performing Arts Academy in Springfield, Missouri. At the age of 14 she had her first pageant class and had a mini pageant, at the conclusion. There was another pageant that she entered locally and did very well. That began her pageant and modeling career. Then we heard about the Cinderella pageant, that was going to be in just a few weeks, and her pageant coach from the Performing Arts School said "She is ready to go , she's got everything prepared so, if you want to enter her, go ahead". She won all categories in her age group. So now they wanted her to go on to the State pageant.

So, we went to Saint Louis, Missouri and she competed in the State pageant. There, again, she came out on top. She did a lot of the talent and modeling competitions as well as the pageant and she did very well, extremely well in modeling and talent. She went on to the national level and at the age of 14, won the national modeling and talent competition held along with the Cinderella national pageant. She won this huge trophy that I have displayed for years. That was her beginnings in the pageants.

From then on she entered several pageants. She was very involved in modeling and dance and danced with the Sonshine Dance Company through junior high and high school years. I became very good friends with the owners of the Dance studio. They became like my brother and sister. We were very close, and I started teaching piano and voice for them at the Performing Arts Academy.

I worked evenings and late at the phone company so I could still get Leslie back and forth to her functions. We grew up together. You know, some people think that as a single parent you can't do all those things, but somehow we managed and got her in all the things she wanted to be part of. I attended the meetings, I attended the dance recitals. There is always a way, not easy, but possible.

I remembered my father always complained about having to come to the recitals and things. He would be the one to come, reluctantly attend, yet brag on me and show pride in me. Then when we got home, tell me how I could have done it better. So, I was determined in my heart that I wasn't going to do that. I wanted to encourage Leslie positively. I stood behind her, went with her, and attended the things, maybe, to the other extreme. I was always available in case she needed someone to drive or chaperone. I arranged my work schedule, whatever I had to do. I was always there to attend with her. I was very proud of her. She was an outstanding student and did very well in school. She was a cheerleader and in several school theatrical productions.

### - *Mother & Daughter*

Besides that, we were very active in our Church, always in choir, and in teaching Sign Language classes. She and I also went together to neighboring nursing homes and we would entertain there from time to time. She would dance, we would sing and I would play the piano, we did some magic, and we shared the gospel. We went there to be friends to those people, who sometimes had no one to come and visit them, or were longing for some attention. It was really neat to have my daughter as really my good buddy and friend through those years.

We became involved in Springfield Little Theatre. Leslie auditioned for several shows and made it. They developed what was called the "H.I.T." theatre (the hearing impaired theatre) and the first time they had it, the lady that was in charge of the interpreters called me. She knew me, and asked me if I would be interested in coming in and interpreting. Through the years I actually ended-up in charge of it. I would audition interpreters and train interpreters for the show. They would do "H.I.T." theatre twice a year, and for those performances they would have the show performed in Sign Language. This was another thing that Leslie and I did together. We often were the partnering interpreters for the shows. We actually had two interpreters per show. The shows were a lot of fun, also a great place for us to share testimonies and show people how we lived and had our involvements with Church.

## *Work - Promotion*

My three years, like I said, turned out to be 15 years in Springfield. During that time my daughter was growing up. I worked all those years for the telephone company, which was my mission field, in my heart I always had the desire for missions, especially from the time I had gone to Jamaica. But the work place became my place of outreach, as the people would come to work, they would seek me out, they knew that I loved God. They knew that I was active at church and they knew that I was an active prayer warrior.

When they had a problem or need, they would seek me out; they would come in, find where I was seated and try to get a seat next to me. If they had any need, they would just seek me out, and I was still, as I had been back through high school, I was someone that people came to seek out if they had a problem or concern. So I was there for them in so many ways and I could look forward to go to work at night and see who was going to seek me out and what we may be able to take before the Lord.

Work was different, I tried to work my way up there and I finally had an opening for relief supervisor. I moved into the position and worked that for several years. I became an active Union steward at work for a few years. It looked like there were going to be some openings in management. They had a night relief manager position coming open, so, they asked if I would like to have it. If I took it I wasn't going to be able to attend my graduation from SMS. I said that didn't matter because I've gone through several graduations.

So, I went on into this management position. I worked that for several months and I went to their assessment center. They sent you there to be approved for management. They said that I came out with one of the highest scores, that they had ever seen and that I was excellent material for management.

Divestiture hit the telephone company. They decided who was going to be AT&T and who was going to be Bell. They also decided that they were very, very surplus in management and indicated that it would be years before there would be chances for people to advance in to full-time management. Even the part-time and my relief positions that I had were probably going to be eliminated. So, I went from looking to a retirement future with this company and moving all the way up in management to becoming not able to go any higher than I was for the rest of my career. I became unsure as to what was going to be my career, because they were also talking about closing offices across the country and eventually that is what happened.

They decided that they were going to close our office, and prior to the office closing they offered me, after 18 years with the company (3 in Ohio and 15 in Missouri), a buyout package. If I didn't take it I would have to go to Saint Louis or Kansas City. I didn't really have a desire to go to either one, so I chose the buyout. I was very unsure at that point what my future was going to be, where I would be, what I would be doing, but again I just moved on and trusted God and God did lead us and direct us.

## *Teaching & The Deaf*

Also through those years I became a substitute teacher in Springfield Public Schools. I could have worked every day between music and Deaf Education. They had called me at one point, in Deaf Education, to fill in for a lady that was going on pregnancy leave. I was teaching during the time of the Challenger explosion. The Deaf Education classrooms had televisions. I remember that day; folks would come in and watch. The TV was on that day, all day long, we were watching the events and the re-caps. That day had a great impact on all of us as we saw it, right before our eyes, as they re-played time after time on TV. We taught about the space program and talked about it, how everyone felt about it.

One year I was hired to teach a deaf class full-time. There was a conflict with another one of the teachers in the deaf program. I think she probably thought that I was going to maybe take over or that I knew more or something. Anyway, I taught that one year. One of the students that I had worked with (let me share this small example with you) was ready to go from elementary to junior high school level. His parents spoke to school officials who were trying to convince them that as he went to junior high that he should be put in a special classroom. They said he would not be able to handle the regular classroom.

Working with this child, knowing and understanding his background, I knew that he had a few problems, a few areas that he had to work on, but that he was very intelligent, very capable. I believed he would be able to make it in a regular classroom as long as he was provided an interpreter to go with him. Being put into a special classroom would give him a special degree when he was through school. That would change his possibilities for college.

I encouraged his parents, after working with them in the summer, to go to the school officials and tell them that their requirement was to have him placed into a regular classroom with an interpreter, at least on a trial basis, to see if he could handle it. I tutored him that summer. His parents had no extra finances, but I knew he needed some work in math and spelling skills. I tutored him at home, at no charge to his parents, simply because I had faith and believed in what he could do. That fall, totally against the school board recommendations, they placed him into a regular classroom with an interpreter and that's how he began junior high.

He went through junior high and high school with an interpreter. He was on the principal's honor role the first year in junior high and maintained that high status through his entire junior high and high school years. He played sports and was very active in other school activities. He graduated and went on to college. I believed in my heart that we, so many times, hold somebody back because we label them with handicap and we actually put the handicap on them, we keep them from their full potential. My heart broke for that child as he was being labeled. I didn't want to see him be one of those labeled and put aside. And so I went to battle along with his parents. His parents were also Christians and we prayed and we sought God, and we got proper schooling for him.

When I was beginning to teach Sign Language and interpreting at the college. I got a phone call at home one day from a woman who said that her daughter was deaf. They had been in the oral program for a while, but her daughter definitely needed total communication, she was in the public school. And her mother was very frustrated because she was not able to communicate that much with her daughter. Her daughter did sign but they did not use it at home. Her husband objected.

It was one of those deals where he didn't want folks to really realize that his daughter was deaf, and he wanted to cover up the situation, therefore, not to sign. But the mother worked hard to learn Sign. She needed to communicate with her daughter. She could not afford to come and take the classes at college. So, again I volunteered and told her I would come into her home and I would teach her Sign Language. So, I did that, I started going to her home, visit after visit, and teaching her Sign Language in her home. I saw her improve her Signing skills and become excited as she began to communicate with her daughter.

Also they started attending the Church (Cherry Street Baptist) Leslie and I attended and we started a deaf ministry there. The mother became more and more proficient in Sign Language and she became an interpreter on her own. Eventually there was a separation in their family. The mother began interpreting in the public schools and did so for many, many years.

A deaf young man contacted me to interpret for him in traffic court. He had been there before and was sentenced to ARTOP (Alcohol Related Traffic Offense Program). Before sentencing the judge called me into his chambers and asked me if I would be willing to attend ARTOP with this young man so that he could understand everything taught there. I agreed. The young man's sentence was 'to attend ARTOP with his interpreter, *me*'. I was a part of his sentence.

Opportunities time after time; God put in front of me, people needing help, people to work with and they were all a blessing to me. I was often so humbled at the fact that God took me, a little bitty nothing, gave me the intelligence and skills for whatever I needed, to be able to reach out and help other people. But most of all, He gave me His heart, to look at people and see them and their needs as He would. God taught me to think of people from that childlike perspective: seeking, eager to learn.

My pastor at Southside Baptist Church had a sign on his podium that he would have to see every time he spoke, a little sign that said: "**Sir, we would see Jesus**". And I remember seeing it Sunday after Sunday, as I would sit in the choir behind the pastor. That has been my heart, even before seeing the sign; people need the Lord, lonely people on my memory. As I was in different churches, throughout my childhood and growing up, as I taught Sunday school classes and Bible studies, worked with people on various jobs, went to school, and talked with neighbors, everywhere I went I had a heart of compassion for every person that I came across. I wanted to look at them, I wanted to see them through Jesus eyes and feel them through his heart. I believe God granted that to me as he brought these different people across my path and gave me the tools that I needed to help them.

## *Relationships*

We had come through many years without any communication from Leslie's father, and she wanted to know him, she was curious about her father. She wanted to meet him, to know him. I tried to tell her the good things about him. I tried not to tell her my negative thoughts about her father. I was always honest with her and she knew that he had a family. She knew that we had decided that he needed to stay with his family, and that he would stay in Jamaica. I had a few pictures that I shared with her and I told her how he had built and established Churches throughout Jamaica. What a good preacher he was, what a testimony he had.

And those were the kinds of things I tried to instill in her about her father. She had the desire to meet him and to know him and we had no contact with him since Leslie was just about two years old. She had begun to search and it was before the days of all the TV and computer searches they have now. She wrote letters to some of the talk show hosts and some of the TV programs that did talk about seeking and finding lost people. She never had any response and Leslie was so eager to know and find her father. When she was 14 I hired a private investigator, it was very expensive but it was something that was very important to her. I could tell that she needed to know him. I hired an investigator to go search for him.

During those years I had became quite obese. I had been told all my life how big I was, how fat I was, so I was living up to others expectations of me. It was also like a defense mechanism. If I was overweight that would make me unattractive. I wouldn't have to worry about men and their interest. Obesity would protect me from bad relationships. I felt I might be better off to be that way. However to my dismay it didn't seem to work. I had a college professor that made advances towards me and I thought: "Oh! Dear! Fat hasn't hidden me very well." I was for some reason still attractive to people.

I met a man through some business that I was taking care of and we began chatting. As I always do, they ask me something about my life and I related it to what God has done for me or he is doing for me.

And we began talking and he told me how he became a Christian, and had gotten away from things of God. He had been married and had two children, but he and his wife were separated, that they had been separated a couple of times, and that he didn't think it was going to work. So, I just tried to talk to him and share with him the word and my own experiences. He seemed to enjoy talking to me. So often when I saw him during business he would take extra time and we would talk. And one day we decided to have dinner together. By this time, now, he was divorced (so he said).

He seemed interested in getting back to a life centered on God. I liked him; he was a lot of fun, joked around a lot, very interesting. So we began a friendship and we started having lunch often. I worked evenings at the phone company, so I wasn't available in the evenings to date. We would meet through the week for lunch. After a little while I wondered why he never asked me to do anything on the week-ends: on a Saturday or Sunday. Although I still worked on those evenings, during the day I was available. I had invited him to church several times, he was supposed to come, but never seemed to make it. He seemed like he really wanted to come.

This went on for actually over a year and I had grown very fond of him and I began to like him very much. I began to respect him, because he respected me and he never made advances towards me, he never came on strong. He really respected me, where I came from, and where I was in life, how I centered my life on God, served people and raised my daughter. We drew closer and closer over a few years period and drew a little more intimate as time went on. I was beginning to think that there might be a future with this person, that I might be able to establish a life with him. We grew our relationship gradually, slowly. Although we never said it, I thought that he might be thinking of a permanent relationship.

After he had won my heart and I realized that I had fallen in love with him, I began to wonder why things were not advancing. One day I learned from one of his employees that he was back with his wife. He had actually gone back a short time after we started seeing each other; he just didn't want me to know it. So, needless to say, I felt betrayed. We had grown into a more intimate relationship. All that time he was back with his wife. He continued with me, knowing how I felt about God and following biblical principles. I saw him from time to time; we were always good friends and chatted. That did not do much for my ego since I had grown to love and care for this person, and then to realize I had been so deceived.

And once again, I felt very much alone. I had God, trusted God, believed in God, but as far as relationships I seemed to be a failure. Anyway, after that, I turned to food and got quite obese and finally came to the point where I was going to have my stomach stapled, because I was to the point that I had to do something. I was having problems with my feet; I had literally worn out the balls of my feet and some nerves because of carrying all that weight around. I had foot surgery, to clip a nerve in the foot that had been very painful. When I went in for that surgery they discovered a spot in my lung, and wanted to know if I smoked, which I never had.

They watched the spot; they thought it may be cancer. A couple of years I went through tests, first it was monthly, then every couple of months and finally every six months, and then finally yearly checking to make sure this thing didn't change or grow and finally they determined that it was probably a scar tissue from something – never knew for sure.

And now, I had recovered from all that and I was going to have my stomach stapled. I read about the surgery. I knew someone that had it done, so I knew it was quite dangerous the way they had to clip and reconnect the intestine and all like that. But I felt at this point desperation to lose the weight. I had tried all the diets and the exercises and they would work for a time, or momentarily. I even started a 'fat club' at work; we lost several hundred pounds among us, collectively. But invariably, I gained back what I had lost, and I reached my peak. So, I felt like, if I was going to be effective and healthy in the future (I was in my thirties). I needed to just get this taken care of. It was affecting my body, my life.

So I scheduled surgery to get my stomach stapled which was quite a serious surgery. I went in and had it done. During my week in the hospital the investigator showed up and told us that he had located Leslie's father.

He was living in New York, had his own business, and had been separated from his wife for about five years. The investigator had made contact with her father and her father wanted to see us. Two weeks after my leaving the hospital, we went to New York to see him. Leslie (now 14), of course, was excited to go and meet her father. We spent a week there, seeing some sites, but mostly time for her to get to meet and know her father.

After all that time and no contact, he was very anxious to renew the relationship with me. Immediately he wanted us to pickup as though we had not ever separated and I said that I could not. After all those years of his turning his back and ignoring Leslie, and I had grown in God and understanding my life and purpose, I could not have a relationship with him now. Leslie and I went to bed one night, and we were discussing the situation. I told her how I felt and she agreed. She knew my life was settled with God. And I did not believe that was what God wanted us to do, particularly after that amount of time. We had a good visit. It was good for her to meet him and get to know him, and of course, we returned to Springfield, back to our 'normal' activities.

On her 16th birthday, Leslie was involved in a play at Springfield Little Theatre. So, I invited the entire cast to come to the house after the show that night for her birthday party. Leslie's father had contacted me just the week prior. He wanted to come and be a part of her 16th birthday. So I told him it would be all right, he could come and stay a few days over her birthday. I left the theater early that night and went home to finish the preparations. He arrived at the house and was also waiting there when Leslie and her friends arrived from the theatre. So, naturally, she walked in the door, and she spotted her father sitting there, she was all excited, of course, this was the second time in her life that she had seen him since a baby.

She had seen him two years before when we first found him and through those years they corresponded by letter and phone calls. But she had not seen him again until that night. I was a little disappointed because it was her 16th birthday and I wanted it to be special, and it was for her, but I felt like his being there robbed me of the joy, after all this time, all of a sudden he showed up. I had to deal with that, get over that. I didn't hold it against him, but yet, I felt a little deprived because of the situation.

She also started dating; she had a fellow she liked very much. She met him at school and they became good friends but he went on and was dating someone else. She was very hurt by that, you know, the teenage thing, but she never forgot him. Then she didn't date for a while. She was involved in a lot of things: theatre, dance, modeling, pageants, and church, Sign Language, all the things she did. She was very busy, but she stayed in contact with him through a couple of years, and really didn't seem to have much of a desire to date anyone else.

We came down towards the end of my tenure with the telephone company. I had lost 90 lbs after my stomach surgery. We got through the meeting with her father. I had made several advances with work and found out I could not go anywhere with it due to divestiture. I had been involved with all the Sign Language things, and the music things, I finally completed my schooling and graduated with my Masters degree.

I really never felt bad about being single. I often felt it would have been nice to have a husband, a 'normal' family life. Mother's Days were particularly a hard time for me, and I think I gave my daughter the wrong impression about Mother's Day. I didn't like Mother's Day. Every time we went to Church we had people in our Church give flowers to one another that you honor as mothers. But Mother's Day was the one day out of the year that I thought it not fair that there was not a man in my life.

As a child growing up, my father always helped us children to make Mother's Day special for my mother. I just felt like it was a day that the husband should honor his wife as a mother. Consequently, that was one day out of the year that I felt extremely alone, very much alone. Being single enabled me to do many things in life that I could not have done if I had been married and had a larger family.

## *Holidays*

Another thing was the holidays during Christmas and New Years. I always decorated; I had all kinds of people into my home. People from work, people from Church, and people from school, particularly if there were people out there that were separated from their family or alone.

I prepared all kinds of great food and served treats, I would make presents. Because of that everybody thought: "Oh! Karen loves the holidays, she gets into them, and in fact it was a blanket, covering the fact that I missed my family at that time, because again as a child growing up, the holidays were very much a family affair.

Each year as I prepared and planned for the Holidays, I would get everything ready, see what Leslie's desires were for Christmas, what she would like to have, who she would like to visit with. We would go see Santa Claus. One time we had Santa Claus come to the house. Just as the girl did to Peter in the Bible as he knocked on the door, she closed the door and came running to tell me that Santa was out there. Some years for Christmas we had the toy that had to be put together and I'd be up late getting hidden items or putting things together and doing the late wrapping and all of that.

I always liked to do the shopping early. I hated to go into the malls and main shopping areas after Thanksgiving with all the Christmas hustle and bustle. Consequently, I was very well known at work for having my Christmas shopping, done before Thanksgiving. That was always my goal, to be finished with my Christmas shopping before Thanksgiving time.

I did a lot of my shopping at Silver Dollar City; it was one of my favorite places, not far from us in Branson, Missouri. We would buy season passes each year and I would take Leslie several times through the year. Our friend, Patty, would go with us a lot (she was a lady that I worked with). We would go to Silver Dollar City and as I would see some things that I thought "Oh! So and so would like this." or "This would be good for whoever!" I was fortunate that I came across things throughout the year for Leslie and for all those I bought gifts for.

As we would go somewhere and we would see something that she liked and I couldn't afford it at the time (sometimes I could, but I would tell her that I couldn't get it at this time) and I would sneak back in and get it and hold it for Christmas or that kind of thing. Lots of times when money was tight, and we had several years when finances were tight, presents were slim at holidays. Sometimes it took me all year to save up for something that Leslie wanted.

One year, she was getting older; I remember making her a book: "Things I promise I will never get you for Christmas." It was kind of a unique idea I had seen in a magazine. She had a lot of fun with it. So there were a lot of things that we did that can be done to make the holiday special and they can be done without a lot of funds. I made a lot of gifts, I shared things and we gave things, and invited people into our home. I made things inexpensively, out of felt, made things out of baby food jars, or made lanterns out of dishes. The lanterns were made from old dishes that I had gotten at a garage sale. I would make ornaments out of clothes pins, just all kinds of little things that were inexpensive.

I tried to share the spirit of giving and I had to do it in a very economic way. I always enjoyed doing those things. A lot of times I would make those summer projects when we were out of school. We would work on making things together. It was a fun thing to do and a way of sharing that we always enjoyed.

I had a lot of birthday parties for Leslie, as she was growing up. We would do the pizza thing and special place parties and the skating parties and all of those fun things. We would have her friends in; we were often sharing our home with old and young alike. We would have groups from Church, different groups from school, different groups from work. We just enjoyed having people in our home.

## *More Life - Loss - Green Peppers*

During my first few years in Missouri I not only had the problem with my father having his heart attack, but, I experienced the death of my grandparents. One grandmother, then another and then my grandfather, all died in a very short period of time. I think it was within a year, or a year and a half, they all passed away. We always looked forward to the phone call to or from home. Leslie always enjoyed those phone calls. My father was the only real male figure in her life. She knew some of the men from Church and friends. She didn't know anyone as a father figure. We kept family ties through weekly phone conversations and our yearly visit.

# LIFESONG - MY SYMPHONY

I could always get a vacation in January. We would usually go right after New Year and we were usually caught in a snow or ice storm on the way back. Then in the summer time sometimes we would go, but a lot of times I could not get summer vacation.

My school tuition wasn't very high. It was very minimal, but still, it was over and above our expenses. In the summer there were times when I had to go ahead and pay those. Sometimes we were low in funds for a few months. During those times a lady at work learned that I liked green peppers. She raised her own vegetables, had her own garden. Every summer she would come and bring me bell peppers, tomatoes, cucumbers, just things out of her garden. I would buy a loaf of bread and we would have green pepper sandwiches, or tomato sandwiches. So we were often sustained for several weeks during the summers on green pepper sandwiches.

By the way - I love green peppers, anyway you fix them. I like peppers on things, in things, cooked, raw, and it's a good thing that I do, because it's how God provided for us and sustained us during that period of time.

In Missouri in 1984, I began an extensive study on the 666 system. It was something that I was really interested in: Revelation and things that were going to happen in the future, and see how prophecy was coming to pass. I began reading a lot of books, listening to any messages that I could find on the subject, studying everything the scriptures had to say about it and, as a result of that I became very convicted financially. Through those years of raising Leslie I had good credit. But because of life's bills and the extra things I wanted Leslie to have, all the good things, right things, you know, in school and dance and all of that. Consequently I had gotten credit cards and ran them to the max. I had a new car and I sat there in 1984 and came under this conviction.

I realized I was a single parent, $25,000 in debt. I woke up to that mountain of debt. I knew there was no way I was going to climb over and out from under, or around or through this mountain. I paid what I could, when I could. I also had some medical bills. It seemed like every time I was getting ahead, something else came up that needed extra money, and then came the time when I had to leave the phone company. I did not make the same amount of money even 15 years after that. God dealt with me about finances and I began working on that part of my life. It took years to catch up the loose ends.

My church showed the Mark 4 series having to do with Revelation, the end times. I even bought copies and shared them with people through the years and I just feel we need to be aware of the fact that those days are coming. We think we have problems, we think we have worries or concerns or financial burdens or relationship problems or physical problems, whatever, but we have no problems at all when we look at the problems for those left here and lost. If we really understood what will happen during that time, we would not hesitate at all to share with people and be a witness to them, making sure they have a definite understanding of Jesus Christ and a relationship with Him. We would want to help them keep from going through those end times.

The summer that I left my job at the phone company Leslie was preparing to be a senior in high school. We were heading that summer to Miami, Florida for another Cinderella competition. Leslie, once again, won big in the modeling competition. Every time we would go to Florida, we would stop by my brother's who lived in Sanford, Florida. While we were there I called several school districts, got applications and even had a couple of interviews. One school I interviewed with for a Deaf Education job was so impressed with the fact that I had my daughter coming with me who would be a senior in high school and was involved in music, drama and a good student. They wanted Leslie in their school.

So, they called me and they really encouraged me to be there. There had been an interview session at Southwest Missouri State earlier that year for people who had graduated with their Masters degree and I had gone to that. I had interviewed with a lady from that same school district where I now applied and was interviewing. When I called letting them know I was in the area, they were thrilled to have me there. As a result of the interviews I could have had jobs in three or four districts in Deaf Education and there were also a lot of possibilities in music.

Besides all that – we loved going to Disney World.

# LIFESONG - MY SYMPHONY

# CHAPTER 7: FLORIDA

We began discussing all this as we returned to Missouri. I told Leslie that I felt she was a senior in high school and I didn't want to take her out of that school before her senior year. But she said she didn't think that would bother her; she liked Florida and she would like to come to Florida. She would like to graduate in Florida, she didn't mind leaving at that time, and she was ready for some changes. I kept contact with the school districts in Florida. I was offered a couple of jobs and decided to take one in Brevard County.

I took a position as Itinerate Hearing-Impaired instructor, which meant I would travel from school to school and work with Deaf students with varied backgrounds, some used Sign Language, and some used oral methods, all of them used T.C. (Total Communication). The job I took was in the school district that wanted my daughter in their high school. It just so happened that we moved into an apartment and moved in an area placing her in their high school, they were thrilled.

She became very active her senior year, active in chorus and she seemed to have a good time, met some new friends and seemed to be enjoying things at school. One of my students went to that high school, so I was there a couple of times a week. I got to know the music director and found a Youth for Christ friend of mine from Ohio was actually accompanist for the choral department. Her son also attended the school and was in Leslie's class. I became an accompanist there also. That gave me more opportunity to be involved in Leslie's activities. I used to go along and be the extra driver for the music competitions and things like that. The music director and I became good friends.

In the last few weeks before leaving Missouri, Leslie had begun dating a young man from our church. I liked him very much, he was very talented, very enthusiastic, an exciting young man. He was a few years older than Leslie, but I didn't mind that, because I knew his Christian standard and background. So, I thought it was a very good match. Then, of course, we left, not long after they began to date. They wrote back and forth that first year. At Christmas time, he came to visit and asked her to marry him.

# LIFESONG - MY SYMPHONY

Now, I really didn't have any objections to her marrying him, but they wanted to get married as she finished high school. He had been through college and did all the traveling with the band, with the choir and all of that and I didn't want her to miss out on those opportunities. So, I was hoping they would wait.

I enjoyed my work very much that first year. There was one little guy that had several things wrong with him. He was not hearing impaired but he couldn't speak and had no communication skills. So, I started working with him in Sign Language and speech. He became very ill and had to leave the public school setting. I was assigned to him as a home school teacher which meant that I went to his home and instructed him there with his mother and his family. I tried to find ways that he could communicate. I tried to use things that he was surrounded by and familiar with. And I remember his mother was so thrilled with the progresses as he began to communicate, they began to communicate with one another.

I remember the time they took him back to Shands Hospital in Gainsville, Florida and the mother told me the doctors were so impressed with the fact that he was able to say "My name is Brandon". That was just another of those times in my life that I just thanked God for the tools and ability he had given me, that I could help other people to grow and progress and learn.

One of my greatest desires was for Leslie to grow up, get married and have a family, because that was something that I was not able to give her. I wanted for her to be able to have that kind of relationship and that kind of a future. I also didn't want her to miss out on those fun years in college, the time of learning, growing and maturing. She got engaged and continued writing back and forth to the young man in Missouri. Leslie was involved in her school activities, had been in a couple more pageants that year, and several music things.

I went to the little Church that prayed me to Florida. When my brother knew that I was thinking about coming, he went to his Church and told them about me. When he told them of my involvement in music and involvement in Church activities, they desired to have me come and be a part of their Church. So, they began to pray that God would lead me there and give me a job near them. We visited a couple different Churches, but that was where Leslie and I decided to attend. That, of course, was in Orlando, so we were traveling back and forth all the time from Titusville to Orlando to attend Calvary Church and church functions. We were there for several years. I played the piano and my brother and I worked with the choir: he led the choir and I played and gave some direction as well. We introduced some new music and were quite active and involved in that. The Church was great as far as lifting us up in prayer and being concerned about us and caring about us. The Church went from meeting in just a small dance school to moving into their own building. God blessed Calvary Church.

After the first year teaching the hearing impaired in Brevard County, we were making so many trips back and forth to Orlando. Leslie was going to attend college at the University of Central Florida, which was in Orlando. We were attending Church in Orlando; Leslie was going to a modeling/talent agency in Orlando. (She had an opportunity to make an appearance on "Super Boy".) So, I thought that the next school year I would see what openings they had in Orlando, and possibly we would move that way. My brother lived in Sanford and we didn't live very close to him either.

I started checking in Orlando and I heard of a high school music position that was open. It sounded almost too good to be true: it was a school music position, they hadn't had a vocal teacher for five years, the band director had been teaching one choir class and that was it. They also wanted to develop a keyboard program there; they had obtained this special grant to develop this keyboard program. When they learned of my background - playing instruments, the keyboard, and being certified in vocal music, they hired me.

When Leslie was getting ready and getting prepared for college, I was preparing for a new job in Orlando. During that summer we moved to the small town, Winter Garden, Florida, where we had some folks from our Church who were going away for a few months up north and they wanted someone to stay in their home. We put our things in storage and moved in there while we were in the interim period between Titusville and Orlando. From there we moved into our townhouse apartment in Orlando, not far from where I was teaching and also not too terribly far from the college that Leslie was going to be attending. That worked quite well for us. I went back and forth to work from there, both to teach school and to Disney. The first year that I was there I learned about a job through my cousin who worked for Walt Disney World Security. She was a security shopper. It was like the mystery shopper, where you will go into an area and you will check everything for: safety, quality, cash handling, proper costuming and dress, all of those things. I started in that position, I worked in that part-time position for 8 1/2 years.

At the school, I developed a music program. By the end of the year we were invited to sing at Walt Disney World which was quite a compliment and accomplishment. A lot of the local school choirs liked to attend and participate in things at Disney but all were not accepted or offered the opportunity.

I really enjoyed the first year teaching there at the high school. I had a good time with my students, I developed ensembles, and we traveled throughout the city of Orlando at Christmas time, presenting a special Christmas program that was well accepted across town. We were invited to come back and then, of course, after the thing that happened with Disney, that was a great accomplishment, I took them to competition. We didn't do extremely well in the solo ensemble contest. But, this was our first year out and it was at least getting our feet wet into the competition aspects. We also had the largest musical that was ever produced in the school. We did it that spring in conjunction with the drama department.

There were a lot of accomplishments in that short year, also a lot of opportunities to share witness with my students. I developed a women's chorus and out of that group there were several from an area home for troubled teens, teens without family or with poor family situations. Some of them as young teens already had babies or were pregnant, of course, not married. It gave me an opportunity to share, to witness and talk about God, to help them through those kinds of things, as I had gone through. It gave an opportunity to meet great people and talk to them and share some things from my own life experiences.

I made special friends with one of the teachers. She and I realized that we were both Christians, so we prayed together, talked about how we felt that Satan was really attacking that part of the city, the city of Orlando altogether, but particularly in this school area. A year or two later she got married and asked me to play at her wedding. Her wedding was at Florida Shores Church. It was my first introduction to the church. Then I began to visit there from time to time.

The first year that I was working at Disney and at the school, but still not as involved in near as many things and activities as I was involved with in Springfield, Leslie was in her first year of college. I began feeling more and more tired. It seemed like it took more and more energy for me to do so few things, when I had done so many things before, and still had energy to spare. I began to get concerned about it, started to have a few physical problems pop up, and just not feeling well. Leslie and I had talked about it, just not quite sure what was going on with me.

Now, from the time I moved to Florida, I had taken a considerable cut in pay and the amount of money that I was making was not what I had made before. I had the bills I was trying to clear up and once again, I found myself in quite a spot because I was still under the conviction to get these bills paid for, and now I am making a lot less money. So, consequently I started getting behind things. I would pay one thing one month, another thing another month. My brother assisted me with the purchase of a car because the car we had moved to Florida in was an older car and was having problems.

I liked Florida and all the people that I met and Leslie seemed to be doing well in school. The boyfriend that she had had in high school in Missouri had relatives in the central Florida area and he came to visit her. They decided that they might want to try to get back together. She broke her engagement and began corresponding again with the old boyfriend. Well, he was making plans to come to Florida to go to college, so things were looking good. I thought she would be here going to school and he was going to come here and go to school. Out of the blue she announced he wasn't going to come here, he was going to stay in Springfield, and therefore she was going to leave school, leave Florida, and return to Missouri.

## *Project Rock*

During the year I taught in Orlando, some gentlemen came to my class and visited. They told us about a group they were starting through the Volunteer Center of Central Florida called *Project Rock*. It was going to be a song and dance group of high school and college students which was going to do different performances around the City of Orlando to promote volunteerism. I announced it to my students who went to the audition and some made it. My daughter went as a college student to audition. She made the group, and I began working with them as an assistant director. I remained an assistant director with them as long as the group was functioning. Leslie became a featured dancer and even a soloist with the group. They performed at the opening of Universal Studios and various places around the City of Orlando. It was a great experience.

## *Family Ties*

Right after I moved to Florida I had a reunion with a cousin of mine. I hadn't seen her for probably 20 years. They had lived in Chicago during the years that I had lived in Ohio. They were a couple of my cousins that I didn't see as often as I saw the others. It turned out that she lived in St. Cloud, Florida. We made a contact and we got together. It was great reuniting with her and then also her parents. My aunt and uncle had moved here as well, so, when my mother would come to visit she would also go and visit her brother. It was part of the family feeling all over again. It was nice to know that there was family nearby.

Also, she had a daughter the same age as Leslie, so they became friends. It was my cousin who worked for Disney and introduced me to the job there. Later, both our girls worked as shoppers also. So, the four of us all worked together for a while, and that was very nice. Leslie worked there as she was going through her first year of college.

## *Another Job Ends - Leslie Leaves*

At the close of the school year came time to renew contracts. For the next year I had prepared a plan to schedule the classes according to interest and ability. That would give better opportunity to those who wanted to use their talents. This was my second year teaching in Florida and it took three years to become tenured in Florida. I went in for my contract renewal and the Principal told me they were not going to renew my contract. No explanation was given nor did an explanation need to be given when a teacher was not tenured. It was hard for me to understand because of all the progress we were making, all the things we had accomplished throughout the year. We had a lot of problems because it was a new program. We had to build the program. I got classes and everything set up and re-arranged for the following year that was going to be really great. I was looking forward to it, to the things that we were going to be able to do and the way we were going to be able to grow and enhance the program throughout the next year. Now, all of a sudden, I had no job.

Later, talking with someone in the administration office of the school district, they informed me that it had nothing to do with me personally, or with the work that I had done, but the particular school that I taught in had a need for minority teachers and they hadn't met their minority quota. They had someone apply in the music field that was of a minority character so they decided that they were going to hire them and put them in my position to fill that quota. There I was, without my full-time job.

Leslie was going to leave school here and return to Springfield. She thought that she would get a job, and with a job, get herself a car, an apartment and go to school. She would be an out of State student, costing more. She was forfeiting her scholarships and I tried to tell her that whatever job she would get, she would not be able to afford all those things. She was first going to go and stay in her boyfriend's parents home, until she got things worked out.

She left. I was becoming ill at that time and through that summer, in just a couple of month's time, I became extremely ill. I felt like I had totally aged overnight. All sorts of things happened to me.

Not only did I have severe headaches, but also I had severe allergy attacks. I could not tolerate milk products. I was losing bladder control and started to wear Depends. I could not lift my head because of the severe headaches. I couldn't sleep at night and I'd be so tired. I'd drive home from work and I had to sit there 10 minutes or so, till I could get enough energy to get out of the car and go into the house. I developed severe pain in my joints and in my muscles. I had severe muscle cramping and tightening. So many things developed in such a short two months period of time. I made myself continue at the Disney job. I did that 2 or 3 days a week and I think that is what really sustained me because it made me get out and walk, even when it was painful to walk.

I was wondering where I was going to work, feeling very ill, and just not knowing what was happening to me all the way around. And, of course, Leslie was leaving. So, emotionally I was totally distraught. I didn't know where my life was going. I was wondering what God was doing with me and I questioned, "OK! God! I felt like you lead us to Florida, what's happening here? What are you doing with me? What do you want with me here? My full time job is gone, and I came here with financial problems anyway and now it's even worse, now my daughter is gone!" All of these things kept compounding.

## *Darden Restaurants*

One of the men that I worked with in *Project Rock* knew about the loss of my job. He worked with Darden Restaurants. He knew that in their computer area they were looking for people to work on their computer help desk. Because he knew my background as a telephone operator he said, "Why don't you go and apply?" I didn't think of myself as knowing much about computers or working with computers but then I finally stopped and looked at what I had done for the last several years for the phone company. I would sit there and work at computers all day. I applied and I was hired. I started to work that fall for Darden Restaurants' computer help desk and, of course, all the while I continued my part-time job with Disney.

I started in the fall, and through the next couple of months, the physical attacks on my body just kept compounding, compounding, compounding, and by that Thanksgiving, I didn't know from one day to the next if I was going to be able to get out of bed in the morning. I would wake up and sometimes would take a half an hour before I could move enough without hurting too much to get out of bed. I lived in a townhouse with an upstairs and it hurt me so much to go up and down the stairs, that I would get everything I would need in the morning and I would take it downstairs and just make one trip a day upstairs and downstairs.

When I came in from work, a lot of times, I would just collapse on the couch. Collapse, yet not able to really go to sleep, so it was just back and forth and just getting worse and worse.

## *Chronic Fatigue Syndrome*

I had gone with a friend of mine from Church, to visit other Churches on Sunday evenings. Our Church didn't have a Sunday evening service. This one Sunday evening, we were going to visit this Church, and I said: "You know! I would like to go, I feel so worn out. It takes so much energy for me to get ready to go anywhere." And we got to talking about it. We did go that evening. As we were talking that evening, I shared how horrible I felt and all of the things I was going through. She said to me that she had a cousin that had Chronic Fatigue Syndrome and how it sounded very similar. I had seen something on television and I was already suspecting that I may have Chronic Fatigue Syndrome.

She said that she would talk to her cousin and see if she could get me some information. She brought me some paperwork on Chronic Fatigue. As I read it, looked at the symptoms, began to check them off, I had nearly everything that they listed as a symptom for Chronic Fatigue Syndrome. I had just about all of them in some form or another. A Christian lady had written the paper. The lady had listed her name and number at the end of the paper so I called her and spoke to her on the telephone. There were only two doctors in the area that dealt with Chronic Fatigue and she told me about the doctor she went to. He was a Christian and he was in Ocoee, Florida.

I telephoned and made an appointment for the week after Thanksgiving. It came down to Thanksgiving week and I felt so horrible. I didn't feel like I could move at all. I was making myself get up and go to work, but that is all I was doing. I would go to work, come home, collapse, and then go to work again the next day, and I was not very effective at work either. I was so worn out and just felt horrible all the time. So, I didn't know if I would make it through Thanksgiving and I honestly felt that, if I would live through the week until time to go to the doctor it would be a miracle. I did live, and of course, the next week I got to the doctor. He and his wife worked together. She had had Chronic Fatigue Syndrome and had dealt with a lot of the medical people not wanting to acknowledge this as Chronic Fatigue Syndrome. Doctors would deal with the individual symptoms, rather than the overall problem.

They would deal with one symptom and sometimes the things that they would use to deal with one, would cause another area to flare up, or it would be working against something else. One medication that would help one symptom would be detrimental to another one of the body's problems or symptoms. After several years of trying to find some help for her, they came across somebody that doctored with homeopathy.

My appointment was with them both for the exam. They did a very extensive computerized exam. I was there for several hours. They tested me and found many organs involved and several things wrong. They acknowledged that I was dealing in fact with Chronic Fatigue Syndrome and on the verge of a total immune system collapse. They gave me a dose of a natural substance and then I was going to start taking various herbs. They told me that within three months I would feel better and, in three years I would realize just how sick I had been and would wonder just how I really made it. I really got there just in the nick of time. Had I not gotten there when I did, it wouldn't have been much longer till I would have had a total collapse. I thanked God for leading me to the right doctor at the right time. I started healing immediately.

My daughter was gone and all of a sudden there was no communication from her. Just know that a mother's heart was broken. I went six months without hearing from my daughter. I prayed for her constantly and had to believe God had His hand on her and that she was alright – the worst time in my life, the empty heart not knowing if your child is dead or alive, or safe, or in trouble. So, I was not only dealing with illness, with a new job, with financial problems, but the biggest heartache was; the child that I loved, the blessing that I had received, (and we were so close when she was growing up) was not only gone from me but I was not hearing from her. I could not understand why God was allowing these things to happen. I would be daily praying for her, lift her up and ask God to return her to me, to let her be all right, give her health, give her safety and protection.

## *Praise the Lord anyhow!*

That fall, I was driving to Disney one day and the engine totally burned up in my car. I was near the exit to get off to go to work and pulled over. God sent a man in a tow truck right behind me and he pulled over just after I pulled off the road. He asked me if I needed help. He was on the way to another call, so he towed me off the road. But when he looked at the engine he said: "I have never seen anything like this, the sparkplugs are melted down in to the engine, and it had gotten so hot". So, needless to say, my car was a total ruin on top of everything else. So, I felt everything was working against me. It was one of those times in my life when I said: "OK! Satan! If you are trying to get me, you might as well forget it!! Because I am still going to trust and believe God and I want God still in control of my life, I still loved God, I still worship and praise God in spite of my circumstances, and I still prayed and read my Bible". I said, "You can't just take me down!"

I related so many times then, and in other times of my life to Job and David (Bible Characters). I felt I lost so many things there, at that moment of my life. I had lost my job, lost my daughter, lost my car, but yet I knew I didn't lose God. Somehow I knew a thread of hope was still there and God was still there looking out for me. I just had to keep faith and believe that God was working all things together for good to me, who loved him. I just was going day by day and was at least improving physically.

I did start to get better. I ended up working at Darden six years, never was I really happy there. I always thought it was going to be short term, but for some reason God just kept me there for a time. There were several people that I had the opportunity to talk with and share with, and of course, I continued at Disney as a part time security shopper.

Through all of my life circumstances I was growing spiritually. After that six months period without Leslie, one day a phone call came and she said: "Mom! Can I come home?" and told me that things hadn't gone the way she thought they would go and she explained some of the reasons why I hadn't heard from her. I said, "Yes!" Of course you can come home." So, that was a thrilling moment, a miraculous answer to prayer. The day she came home I went to the airport to greet her. Some of her friends from Church, college, and that she had worked with all gathered at the airport to meet and greet her as she returned. I knew how the prodigal son's father felt when he returned home (the prodigal in the Bible).

It was good to have her back home as I was recuperating, as I was coming alive again.

## *Leslie Leaves Again*

After Leslie came back, she went back to college. We talked about getting some counseling for her (she thought she possibly needed help to get over everything she had been through in Missouri). We discussed things that happened while she was gone and she began dating again. Then one day she got a phone call from a man she had met actually in the home of her boyfriend in Missouri. He was a friend of theirs and lived in Maryland. He came to see her and he was an older man. He seemed like a nice man, but he was very interested in Leslie and I tried to caution her after what she had gone through, to not jump into anything again.

But, needless to say before very long, they were engaged. He moved to Florida, just to be near her, to win her. Then he had problems with his job in Florida so he decided to go back to Maryland. When he did, they decided that Leslie was going to go with him. So, once again, she was going to leave school and leave home.

Leslie went to Columbia, Maryland with her fiancé. They eventually got married there. I didn't know when she was getting married. I wasn't part of the wedding. I didn't know until after they had gotten married. They came to Florida that following year, in October, and told me that they had gotten married. They also told me that they were expecting a child. That was easy for me to accept.

I was disappointed because there were things that I had hoped for her. I wanted her to finish college and enjoy school activities and have fun and enjoyment with that. She also dropped out of the pageant system. She was preparing for the Miss America system, and everybody always told her how perfect she would be for Miss America. It was her choice and her decision and I had to accept it, I didn't fight it. But I expressed that I thought she was too young, she still needed to recover from the Missouri situation. I was disappointed that she was missing out on some of the most precious years and times of her life.

I had seen them that October for a weekend. They called me and asked if I would like to come when the baby would be born. I had made arrangements at work, around the time that the baby was due, in late January, I was going to try to take off and go, be with her for a week or so. While I was at work one day, in a meeting, I returned from the meeting and got this message: "Hi Grandma!" I said: "What?" They said: "Your daughter called, she had a baby!"

I just talked to her, the night before; she was going to the doctor the next morning and thought it would be a few weeks yet. Needless to say, I got things together and left that weekend, went, and spent a week with them. Things were strained for the first few visits with my son-in-law, we got past it through the years and I had always loved him and thought of him, really, as my own son. I think I had to convince him because he thought I was objecting to him. I returned and went on with my life in Orlando working at Darden, working at Disney, still not feeling well, but not as bad as I felt before.

## *Pool Ministry*

Also, during those months, while Leslie was gone, I was feeling so ill a lot of times, I would go out those days and make myself swim in the swimming pool, because I felt like; even if it hurt so bad in my joints and everything, I felt that if I didn't move and make myself exercise in some way that I was just going to lock up physically in my body. So, I would go out to the swimming pool after working all night at Darden.

I would get out my little floater, have a paperback copy of the Bible and that's where I would do my Bible reading. I would do all that before I would go in and go to sleep, or when I would get up. That led to opportunities to witness to several people that would be around the pool. One of the big questions was, "Oh! What are you reading?" I loved the question because it gave me the opportunity to share. But God started moving a group of people in to our apartment complex that was attending a motorcycle mechanics school and I thought these are kind of an odd sort for me to make contact with. But it seemed like several of these people, and most of them were men, had a lot of interest in the Gospel.

Once they knew what I was reading and sharing, they had a lot of questions. They would seek me out, look for me at the pool, and ask a lot of questions.

I became interested in one of the fellows and we shared quite a bit of time discussing life and God. He had nearly died in a car accident and he felt that God had spared him for a special reason. He was still searching and seeking. We were very attracted to each other and we became involved in a relationship that I should not have. But I liked the fellow very much. It was also a very vulnerable time for me because it was when Leslie was gone and I was feeling so bad and alone. I just felt like there was somebody that would care about me a little bit and take my mind off my loneliness. We had a very wild, crazy fun affair. I knew deep inside it was wrong but my physical desires took over.

He was a great diversion for my problems. When I was with him I forgot about all the messes in my life. He eventually, through his roommate, met another lady that he decided he wanted to date, so he did, and he ended our relationship, leaving me with one more hurt.

At the pool I met another one of the neighbors, who was a young man that had been in trouble a lot of times. He had spent a lot of time in jail, in prison. He had a young wife and a young son and he had grown up with a Godly grandmother, a grandmother who loved God and talked to him about the Lord. His own family situation was not very good and he had a lot of problems in his life. So, he started seeking me out. He would get drunk and get into a fight or something with his wife. Then he would come and talk, be repentant at the time and say he wanted to change. He wanted to get his life straightened out and then he would turn around, and he would do it all again. I had many opportunities to talk with him and share with him. He knew that he was facing some time in jail or in prison. When he went to jail he would call me periodically and I would write and send bulletins from Church and things with scriptures, trying to share the Gospel with him.

## *Jail/Drinking/Drugs*

While he was there, in jail, he met someone else and started talking with them and he told them about this neighbor that shared the Gospel with him. He called me one day and he said that this fellow was really seeking God, that he needed that kind of inspiration. So, I spoke to his friend a couple of times on the phone and then he actually got out of jail before my neighbor. I met him and talked to him. When he first got out of jail he was living in a situation with three or four people who had come from the same background of being in jail, being involved very heavily with alcohol and drugs and street crimes.

God put me in the place where I met a lot of people from this type of background and opened a whole new door for me to reach out and help others. I felt like it was a whole new ministry for me. That God had led me to the motorcycle people and then to this group of people that had been involved with jail, prison, drugs and alcohol.

Many of them, through the years had attended Church with me, some of them regularly for a while, some of them for one or two visits. They knew that when I came into their home I would talk to them, encourage them, they knew that I would pray for them regularly. I would share with them. They knew that I didn't want to take part in any drugs, or anything like that, but they always welcomed me into their homes. I always thought about it as Jesus would go to where they are and he would share with them and talk to them, and He would let them see Him, and that was my goal, for them to see Jesus.

I had to learn some of it the hard way that they are called cons for a reason and they really do practice conning others. I had to be careful. I learned as I said, sometimes the hard way, that they do take advantage and they will con someone into doing something that they feel that they want or need at the time. I had to learn and discern it. I had to learn to be hard and tough sometimes. I would help some of them by taking them into my home or giving them rides, and I had to learn where to draw the line. I had to learn to not be a co-dependent for them.

I had to learn those things because I was such a giver and such a caretaker. I always wanted to take care of everyone, not that I wanted to change anyone because I knew I couldn't change anyone, only God could. But I also knew that I could pray for them. God would sometimes wake me up at three o' clock in the morning, four o'clock in the morning with a particular one or a group of these people on my mind, knowing that they were out there in trouble or danger or doing things that they shouldn't be doing. God would wake me up and say, "Pray for this one!" or "Pray for that one!" It became a fairly regular occurrence for God to wake me and instruct me at a particular time that these people needed to be lifted up in prayer. I have seen tremendous results in some of their lives and changes in some of their lives.

God still brings them to mind from time to time although I don't see them much anymore. I trust that one day they are going to finally realize that their only hope, their only way to escape and get their lives in order, is to turn their lives over to God. I am just praying for that day to come in many of their lives. And God gave me a vision of one day seeing a whole row of these people just sitting in Church, believing and trusting him.

I am looking forward to that day and believing in faith that it is going to happen, because God showed me that it will. It's been an interesting ministry to me. I enjoyed the time of learning, I learned so much about people that come from the street, bad family relationships and had to live on their own, have no family, no one to rely on, and no one to fall back on, if anything happens. When I had my problems, at least I had my Church and my family. I had someone that I could look to. I knew if I lost my place to live or lost my car or whatever, that I would have a place to go, at least a shelter, but these people had nothing and no one.

There were times that I was in some of those places, and I ended up in some unbelievable places. I ended up in the heart of drug areas, sometimes I learned to know who some of the dealers were. I learned how they go about their business. I learned the habits and methods and ways of a drug addict. I learned what alcoholics do from morning until night, how they live, how they survive on that drink from morning till night. I always felt safe and I always felt secure. I felt that God was protecting me and God was leading me and if there were times that I was in places that I shouldn't have been, I realized I needed to get out and I would go and leave the situation. Again, I had to learn these things, learn what was going on around me, what was going on with these people, but God graciously kept his hand on me and guided me, protected me.

## *Amanda's Miracle And Mine (Heart Tumor)*

Through the years God was healing me from the Chronic Fatigue Syndrome. The doctor was right. After three years I realized how sick I had been. However, there was one symptom we could never truly get under control. It was the heart palpitations. They kept returning. That puzzled even my doctor, because we seemed to get most everything else under control. There would be times when some of the symptoms would creep back, the tiredness, the lethargy, the lack of energy, and the fatigue. And when this would happen, from time to time, I would re-dose on major herbs and things like that, and it would help for a while, but then they would come back, particularly the heart palpitations.

After my granddaughter Amanda was born, she was a few months old, and they started noticing some problems in her growth, some changes in the way her head was growing. They went to a pediatrician and they sent her to be checked by a specialist. They found that she did have a problem.

Her skull was growing incorrectly, and if left unattended her head would be deformed. It was growing together too quickly and her brain would not have room to grow. Therefore she would end up with brain damage as well. God had put them in Columbia, Maryland, and again (see how God works) He puts us in the place where we need to be, when we need to be there. John Hopkins University Hospital was very near. Doctor Ben Carson, who was the doctor who developed the surgery that spared Amanda's life, was there, at that Hospital. Just a couple years prior he had developed this surgery. He was the only man to have ever successfully separated twins joined together at the skull.

That is who God prepared for Amanda's surgery. He said that when Amanda would be six months old he would perform the surgery. He also said that she may have to have a series of surgeries, depending on how things grew and the progress that she would make.

Naturally, we began to pray. We had our Churches here in Florida, in Ohio, in Pennsylvania and all across the country praying for her. Things still weren't the greatest for me financially, and I knew it would be difficult to get time off and go when she had her surgery. Once again, it was one of the times when I wasn't feeling extremely well.

My mother and Aunt would come periodically to visit from up north. My mother had come down to visit. One summer day in July we took my brother to MGM Studios. While we were there I was pushing him in the wheelchair. It was very hot and it was just before Amanda's surgery. I often pushed my brother in the wheelchair. We had gone into one of the shows. I began feeling one of what I called my "drain modes" (all of the sudden I would feel super wiped out and drained). I would sometimes have to sit, just take a minute or two, and then I would recoup, be able to go on. Sometimes, I would have to close my eyes, and this began happening more and more frequently, sometimes, several times a day.

I couldn't figure out what was going on. (I had gone back to the doctor but this time nothing seemed to help the heart palpitations.) We went in one of the shows and I felt that would have been long enough to recoup. But as we left there and I started pushing him again, I felt faint. I felt horrible. I felt like I was going to blackout. I aimed for a bench. By the time I got to the bench, I was seeing black. I couldn't see. It was like I was ready to blackout. I sat on the bench. My heart was racing. I felt there was something wrong, that didn't feel quite the same as the heart palpitation I had while I was dealing so heavily with Chronic Fatigue. This time I didn't seem to come back. Other times when I went into my "drain mode" I would bounce back. This time just seemed to linger and I wasn't sure what was going on. Finally, because I wasn't feeling well, we decided to leave and we left for the day.

Monday came and I just didn't feel like going to work. I didn't get my energy back. I called work and I told them that I seemed to have problems with Chronic Fatigue, again, and I wanted to take a day or two off. They called back and asked if I would mind getting a second opinion, because of dealing with Chronic Fatigue. There were only two other doctors in the vicinity, other than my own, that dealt with Chronic Fatigue and I couldn't get to see either one for at least six months. Work asked me, "Since heart palpitations are one of the symptoms, would I consider going to a cardiologist just to get a second opinion?" I said, "Sure!" Work actually set up an appointment and I arranged to go the following week to a cardiologist.

Tuesday I went to the cardiologist and he didn't find anything wrong with my heart. The EKG came back normal, listening to the stethoscope was normal, but because work had sent me, he decided to do this other batteries of tests; he said he expected to find nothing. He felt my heart was OK. Probably it was the Chronic Fatigue I was dealing with, but he would go ahead and run the tests because they had sent me.

The following Thursday he wanted me to come in for these tests, now this was just a couple of days after Amanda had her surgery and she was still in intensive care. I went to have the tests that day and one of the tests was an Echocardiogram. I watched the fellow doing the tests. I could tell there was a problem, something he was seeing. He asked, "How did you get here today?" I explained to him that I had driven, not only that, I was packing, getting ready to move. I had found a new apartment in Altamonte Springs and I was going to move there, I was going to be closer to my brother, closer to a good friend of mine and no longer needed to live close to the school where I once taught. So, I was in the process of moving, as well as my granddaughter having surgery, and then this, whatever was going on with me physically. I knew there was something he was seeing on the screen. I turned and I saw it also. I think he thought that it was a blood clot or something in the chamber of my heart. The doctor was out and he asked me if I could stay until he came back later that afternoon. I said, "No! I am in the process of packing and moving." He said: "I don't think you should do that, can you call someone, to at least, come and get you?" I said, "No! I'll be fine".

I went home, packed a couple of boxes and returned that afternoon for the results. I had a tumor, a rare tumor, growing in my heart. It had gotten so large that it was now filling the one chamber of my heart and when I would go into what I called "the drain mode" was when the heart was beating, the valve was opening and the tumor was trying to push down into the other chamber because of its size. Therefore the valve was not closing properly and that was causing me to have these modes. Apparently, that day when I was pushing the wheelchair I had just overexerted and very possibly it could have killed me that day, and really, every time it had happened. Had the valve not finally closed, it could have killed me.

Anyway, the doctor said that he already consulted other doctors and they wanted me to come in the following Monday and have the surgery. There was one doctor that wanted to perform it. He said that particular doctor was actually anxious to perform it because it was something different, unique, not a normal bypass surgery. However the Doctor wouldn't be available after Monday, he was going on vacation and was going to be a couple of weeks before he would be back.

The doctor told me, " Well, we could have someone else perform it, or you can wait until he comes back, since you got this far, but you would have to be extremely careful". I said, " If my granddaughter is out of intensive care I will go in for surgery, if she is still in intensive care, then I will not". She did very well through her surgery and she did come out of Intensive Care. That Friday I went in for a heart catheterization. I knew I was going to have it, they told me I would need some careful time after.

I was planning to go home that day and finish boxing up, and finish my moving on Saturday and Sunday so I could go into the Hospital Sunday evening and have surgery Monday.

I went in for the heart catheterization. I didn't realize that I had to spend 24 hours on my back, after the catheterization was done, because you couldn't chance that area breaking open and bleeding. I had the heart catheterization and during it I remember talking to the doctor and telling him about my granddaughter. I told him that I should be set for Monday as long as she came out of intensive care; she was expected to come out within the next day or so. I said something about her being in the right place at the right time and that God orchestrates things wonderfully that way. He said: "She is not the only one that is in the right place at the right time, because after all, in this area are some of the best heart specialists in the world". I was also in a good place at a good time for me.

## *Thank you God!*

Over and over and over again in my life, as I said before, God had me in the place where he wanted me. He had me in the churches he wanted me to be in, in the schools he wanted me to be in, and now in the hospital he wanted me to be in. On and on we can stop and look at how God so carefully planned our lives: the big things, the small things and everything if we just realize it. He is in control and whether we yield our life to Him or not He is the one in control.

I had the heart catheterization, and then I packed my boxes and moved them into my new apartment and moved some into a friend's place until I could get out and get situated. I went in to the Hospital that Sunday night to have surgery the following Monday morning. When I went into the Hospital that day, I knew how badly I had felt, and I knew I had served God; I had a good fruitful life. I had done a lot of things in life but never married, and being single I had been able to have a lot of experiences that I possibly would have missed otherwise.

I said to God: "OK!" I was ready to talk to God that night and I said, "I know that I am not all that old, but I had a good life, witnessed and shared, I have been blessed, I had a lot of experiences, I am just ready to come on home." So, I said, "God, I am ready, please just take me on home".

I was going to just really pray that night, before surgery, seeking God to just take me on home and let me be with him for eternity. That night, before I went to surgery, my brother came to see me in the Hospital, and with him came one of my friends that I have been dealing with who had many problems and had come from jail. Someone that I had drawn fairly close to and really was on my heart as someone I was trying to witness to and share with and someone I was really praying for.

He was one of those people that God would wake me up in the middle of the night to pray for. He said to me: "Now, you (as he pointed his finger at me) know what to do, you know how to take care of this, you do it!" I knew that what he meant was not to pray for God to take me home but to talk to God about healing and making me well. I thought: "Well, OK! Maybe God has more of a purpose for me in this life." So, I changed the way I was praying.

I had a good night's rest before surgery. Early in the morning they were prepping me, getting me ready. My mother had flown back in. She was there, my cousin was there, and my brother and my friend were there. They were all there to see me off to surgery. I was praying and telling God that I was ready one way or the other, but if he had more for me to do then, "Once again take my hand and pull me back and let me know what I am supposed to do". I went into surgery and, as I was waking up, I felt a tug on my hand.

That was when I knew that God was bringing me back for some reason, for some purpose. It was that friend pulling my hand and I thought, "God has a reason for me returning back to a state of health and this is one of the people that God wants me to reach." I wanted to reach out and be an example to him and let him see Christ through me. I felt for him what I felt for Alden all those years earlier in Jamaica.

Needless to say, I recuperated and they were very pleased with my recuperation. I had a very speedy recovery. Felt so much better after that was all over and the energy was restored. I had moved and I was in this small apartment. My mother was there with me surrounded by a mount of boxes. I had moved from a fairly large townhouse with two good size bedrooms all jam-packed into a very small one bedroom apartment. I had all these boxes and I had to decide what I was keeping and what I was throwing away, if I was going to store anything and, if so, where? As I was recouping mother and I sorted out the boxes and the mountains and mountains of things and finally got it fairly well situated. I always felt that the place was too small. I didn't have enough room. But I was there. I couldn't do much about it at that point. (I actually ended up staying there 11 years – till I moved into my house.)

Amanda and I did very well with our recovery. Through the years she had to go back for tests, she had to have NO more surgeries – she was a miracle. The doctors had been so pleased with her progress. Her mother and father taught her well, they worked with her, they disciplined her. She is very normal in every way. No complications of any kind other than she has a hard head, because she got the metal plates and things in her head and screws and what have you. They tease her sometimes about having a hard head, but she is a wonderful, beautiful girl. She too has learned to love God because her mother has taught her. I appreciate that the things I taught and instilled in Leslie, she is now teaching and instilling in Amanda.

After my heart surgery I was still working at Darden Restaurants and Disney, still wondering what I was doing at Darden, it wasn't really where I felt I should be. After the heart surgery some things had happened at the Little Church that I went to. I loved the people dearly, but I found they had some problems reaching out to those folks that I was trying to bring to Church and share with. I felt like I needed to be in a place where I could take any one of them and have them feel welcome. I went to visit the Florida Shores Church (that has since then changed their name to Discovery Church).

I visited there again while I was recouping from my heart surgery. I thought, "I will go visit while I am recouping." God got a hold of my heart, literally, spiritually, physically and emotionally at that time. Physically, of course, with the tumor corrected, spiritually, by moving me to Discovery Church where I was to move in brand new areas and just grow in a way that I didn't expect at my age. I felt like

# LIFESONG - MY SYMPHONY

I knew a lot and learned a lot and, little did I know how much more I had to learn and how much more I had to grow spiritually and emotionally. I had to heal through restoration of the things with my daughter, my son in law and family and things; it was a good time of recouping and regrouping in my life. I began to realize that through those couple of years when I was dealing with the heart problem, feeling bad and not knowing why, that was when I had grown vulnerable to some of those people that God had put in my life. Some of them stayed at my home, some of them for a short period of time, some of them longer. I learned a lot about their lifestyle and things going on with them, but I had to learn when and where to draw the line and not be an enabler. It took me years of learning, years of growing, years of healing in all of those areas in my life.

## *Deaf Ministry Ends – 5 Books*

After all those years working with the deaf, after moving to Florida, that ministry seemed to not open up for me. I taught the hearing impaired the first year, than it seemed I had no involvement with the deaf for the next several years. Just prior to leaving Springfield a gentleman who had taken some of my Sign Language classes at the college called me. He was a book writer, an illustrator and the reason why he and his wife came and took my class was because he had been involved in writing a Sign Language book, co-writing it with another author and he was the illustrator for it. He did all the pictures of the book, by taking the pictures of people signing and then drawing the picture illustration from that.

He and his wife decided to take the class to learn a little bit about the language and after studying with me they realized there was more to it than just doing the sign. I had received a call that they were doing another book and asked me if I would be a consultant on the book. Naturally, I agreed and we started that, just prior to my leaving Missouri, but it was not completed before I left. He sent me pages through the mail. We did all the work through correspondence. I have since consulted on a total of 5 Sign Language books. The work kept me involved through the years even though I wasn't working directly with the hearing impaired themselves.

A couple of deaf people came to Church from time to time. God did not open the door there for a deaf ministry.

I stayed involved, God kept me involved in some way through the years and not in the way that I had expected, not with the deaf, themselves, as I had been for so many years. I missed that in a lot of ways but God had given me new areas of ministry, new groups of people to minister to.

## *Donna*

One of the people that I met through this group was Donna. We became quite good friends and she was dating one of the fellows that had been a roommate of Alan. One day we went to court (her boyfriend was in court) and we were sitting there. We began talking. I shared with her how God had blessed me in several ways and she had told me about her grandfather who was close to the Lord, and what a prayer warrior he was and how he prayed for her all the time. She asked me, "How do I know Jesus like you do?" I told her how to accept Christ by asking, inviting Him in and what scriptures to read (John 3:16) when she went home. I had to leave her in the courtroom, because I had to go to work that day.

> *John 3:16*
> *For God so loved the world, that he gave his only begotten Son, that whosoever believeth in him should not perish, but have everlasting life.*

I talked to her that day in the courtroom. She went home and she accepted Christ as her Savior. She called a few days later saying, "I don't feel any different!" I said, "You are not necessarily going to feel any different, but you will see a difference in your life as you trust and believe in God" That was in October. I had invited her and Jeff to Church, but they hadn't come as yet. In January, I was at work one night and I got this call. It was Jeff calling to say that there had been an accident "Can you come right away?" I did go. My friend Donna had been crossing the street and was hit by a car and was airlifted to the hospital with severe brain damage. She was in a coma for several weeks and finally began to recover.

She had many broken bones. She had damage to her skull and her brain. We did not know if she would live, from moment to moment, we prayed a lot for her. I had moments of prayer with Jeff and with people from my Church. I knew in my heart that should anything happen to her, she was in the right relationship with God and things would be fine for her. I shared her experience with Jeff and he began coming to Church with me, he attended for quite a while regularly. As she recuperated I met her parents and communicated with them through the years. I became a liaison between them and Donna. She was in the Hospital for weeks, months. Finally, when it came time for her to be released, she still couldn't return home. She had to go to a nursing home for special care.

Because she had no insurance, some of the conditions, in some of the nursing homes and places that she was put in were deplorable. Some of the care was poor. Some of the treatment was poor. I found it very hard to believe in this day and age some of the treatments and care in those facilities, the condition of the facilities. It just broke my heart for the people that were there. I reached out to some of her roommates. It was just really something.

Through the years she has recuperated enough to be out in a wheelchair. She has great difficulty walking. Her speech is very unintelligible, but yet, I know she loves God. We don't know why God does and allows the things that he does. I do know that her heart and mind were right with God at the time she had the accident.

There were others that God connected me with through that time. Some would call me from jail or regarding other trouble that they got into. I would accept the phone calls and I would talk to them about the Lord. I often sent them scriptures or bulletins from Church. God allowed them to become a real ministry for me, even though it was strange for me to be involved with them. On one hand I was dealing with them and learning about their lifestyle and how they acted.

For example, about some of the criminal activities, the way that the Court system works, the processes that they go through (and some of it is still confusing to me, understanding how it's done and how it works) and how they go time after time and finally reach a point when they do have to pay for the things they have done.

On the other hand, I was working for Security, looking for people that are doing some of the very things that some of these folks had been involved with. I saw both sides of the spectrum and I tried to meet in the middle and realized that they are all people. I know that God loves each and every one of them. He looks at each one of them as an individual, as someone that he loves and cares for. I tried always to look at them with the eyes of Jesus, no matter what they had done. I thank God for the many opportunities and experiences I had shared with them. I thank God for bringing me back from the open heart surgery because I realized, through it all, that God intended for these people to come across my life.

I just trust and pray that I have been an influence to some of their lives. Even if just one has been restored to God, it was all worthwhile.

## *Too Good To Be True*

After the heart surgery I was still working at Darden and Disney. A very renowned business had consulted with me a couple of times through the years regarding legalities for the deaf and hearing impaired and for interpreting possibilities. They came and sought me out. They were looking for someone to commit to a full-time position. I definitely thought I had died and gone to heaven because the position involved Sign Language, hiring a group of people to interpret, and interpreting in the entertainment industry. I would be training and then working in several different shows and performances. I would be in charge of the whole program. They took me through three major interviews, even with a Vice President. Things were looking very good. They wanted to know how soon I would be able to start. They were waiting for the final approval and they asked me how much notice I would have to give to Darden. I went ahead and I told Darden that I would be leaving. All of a sudden things came to a dead halt and I didn't hear anything from them. After two weeks I telephoned them, they told me someone in their major legal department, in another state in another area, had cancelled the whole project. They did not want the liability for those interpreters and me. They wanted to contract out the services instead of doing it within, so they would not be responsible for the liability and all the benefit expenses for the people. Therefore it was ended immediately.

# LIFESONG - MY SYMPHONY

I went back and Darden had already planned on my leaving, they let me go anyway. Once again I sat there without a full-time job.

I still had the part-time job at Disney. That helped to carry me through. I had unemployment for a while. I lost the job at Darden in November. I began a really special time with God. Through the years I had become more involved with my Church Counseling Ministries. I really enjoyed that ministry and I received a lot of training in the counseling field and attended several classes on Pastoral Counseling. I really enjoyed this team ministry that we did in counseling. Without work I had more time to devote to that.

I had also become very active in the prayer ministry at Church. Anytime I was available when they were having prayer meeting or services, I wanted to be there. I felt like God often called me just to pray, not only at Church and for Church, but as I mentioned before, for certain people he would indicate to me certain times or he would bring someone to mind and I knew it was time to pray for them. Many times through the years, sometimes not knowing why, God brought that person to my mind. Other times knowing in my heart that it had to do with illness or maybe with relationship or what have you. God would put these things on my heart and I would know that it was something, someone that I was to pray for.

I was very active in a ladies prayer group. I attended the meetings all the time and their activities. I was very active, of course, on the worship team, and music. I was playing keyboard. At this time our Pastor and I were the only lead keyboard players. I was playing nearly every Sunday. I was very involved and attended all the rehearsals.

I had all of those things happening in my life when I found myself with no full time job. I didn't want to give up all of those areas and activities. I told God I would just be there any time there was anything taking place as long as he provided the way and the means for me.

I was having some difficulties with my car once again. Now, I had a car with 71,000 miles on it. It was the same car I had the engine replaced in when I was without a job before. It seemed like;

once again, the car was plaguing me at a time when I was in a new financial stress. After all these times of financially trying to get through things, I hit another slump. Every time it seemed I would even get close to getting out of the financial slump, something else would happen. Once again, I was at that point. I had gotten so depressed over financial stuff, through the Chronic Fatigue, which I'd go months at a time without recording activities in my checkbook, without checking my balances, without opening mail. Sometimes I would take mail and just stuff it in bags because I didn't want to see the bills and I didn't want to pay attention to them. I was very down and depressed about that. I was never that way with anything else.

It was something that I just wanted to lay aside, because I didn't want to deal with having to figure out: which one to pay, which one to have to call and give excuses to. I just put it aside, thinking tomorrow I would pick it up and do it. For months, tomorrow never came. I had laid things aside and during that time, I had no job. I began to really get convicted about my finances again.

## *Intimacy With God*

I found myself in a place where my brother helped me; people from my church were very wonderful, supported me, lifted me up and helped me as needed, as they could. I had to totally rely on God, and I found myself developing a new relationship with God that I never had before. I never had time for it before because I was busy working, and for all those years Leslie was a small child I was working 2, 3, and sometimes 4 jobs at a time, as well as being involved with all the activities with her, while going to school myself. I was very active in Church Ministries. I did read my Bible some. I did pray and I did listen to tapes, especially in my car, but I didn't spend really intimate time with God.

I started doing that during those days that I was off, without work. I would get up in the morning. It was the first time that I really learned to read and study in silence. Before, I always had to put on worship tapes, quiet tapes. I would be reading my Bible while the tapes are playing, but then, all of a sudden, I learned that, especially with my mind being so

# LIFESONG - MY SYMPHONY

musical, it was disruptive to me and I would often find myself thinking about what was happening in the music. I decided to turn everything off and read in silence. Sometimes I would hear birds chirping, if it was early in the morning, the sprinkler turned on, and rain if it was raining outside. I just started reading in the silence. It started that November. I was determined in the following year to read totally through the scriptures and I wanted to read through various translations. So, I was determined within myself that I was going to do that the next year. I found one of those plans that take you through the Bible within a year and I was prepared to do that. I spent my mornings, sometimes my days, reading and studying in the word, lots of time in prayer, and I would actively praise and worship God.

I used to be one of those who watched TV during the day, I was never home much in the evenings or nights so I did not know much about evening TV, but I knew daytime. I used to watch some of the talk shows; and yes - some of the soap operas. I remember when "_Day of Our Lives_" had their first show, I was in junior-high or high school and I started watching it on and off through the years. I learned to watch soap operas from my Grandma Twigg. She used to watch. I remember "_The Edge of Night_" and "_Secret Storm_" which were two she used to watch. I started watching them at an early age.

And, like I said, on and off all through the years I would watch them. I liked Oprah. But now I learned to not even turn TV on for days at a time. Sometimes I would turn it on early morning or late night just to get the news or to see if there was something that I really needed to know about; otherwise, I wouldn't have the TV on at all. Instead, I would have the praise and worship tapes on, I would be singing and praising the Lord as I would be cleaning, as I would be doing dishes, as I was reading other books, and I read a lot of other materials during that time as well. I started reading a lot of things written by Joyce Meyer, from the ladies of the Women of Faith conferences, and others I would come across, authors or books or things that my pastor would recommend, I was reading.

So, my days were entirely spent reading the word, reading other good materials, studying other things, praising and worshipping. I loved it.

# LIFESONG - MY SYMPHONY

I began to realize that I was developing an intimacy with God that I never had before because of all the time that I was spending on everything else. It is like when you are dating someone, the more time you spend, the more you are together, the closer you draw. That was what was happening to me, even though I have been a Christian for many years and followed God I was just drawing closer and closer to God. I was getting poorer and poorer financially but drawing closer and closer to God and relying on him more and more for everything.

During this time I was drawing closer and closer to God, I took part in other activities as opportunities came up. There was a conference with Joyce Meyer. Some of the ladies from our prayer group were going to go and hear her. It was a Friday morning and that usually was the time that I met with ladies at the Church for prayer. As I said, I was determined that while I was not working and available, I would go and attend every opportunity I could. One day they were going to go to this conference. I wasn't sure I liked this lady and her voice, but I determined that I would go since the prayer group was going that morning. The first thing that hit me was the music that took place that day.

Clint Brown and his worship team from Faithworld in Apopka, Florida were the musicians leading the service that morning. Every song they sang was just for me. Here I am, sitting there, without funds or a job, spending all that time with God, but really, truly being blessed by the music they brought that morning. I knew in my heart by what I was hearing and what I was receiving, what my spirit was feeling from the music that morning, that there was going to be some message there for me. So, as Joyce Meyer came out to speak and present her message that morning, one of the first things she said was that her offices in Saint Louis, Missouri were in a new complex and they were hiring a lot of people.

So, anyone who was interested in a job may pick up an application in the booth outside after the conference that morning. One of the ladies from church looked down and nodded at me and said, "Karen..." So, I did pick up an application, that day, and I did send it in. I was seeking and searching for God and work.  **(They did later call the church for references from Joyce Meyer Ministries but I did not get hired there. God knows where He wants us all the time. Not my time yet)**

The words that she had to share that morning were just for me. God gave her words that I needed to hear. They fit my situation at that time as so often I had seen God do through the years. Not only did I listen to her and totally change my mind, my attitude from what it had been just that morning when I started out, but I wanted to go back the next day and see if God had some more words there for me.

## *Tell Your Story...*

I began remembering thoughts and feelings that God had impressed on my heart through the years. I just felt that God had said over and over to me, through several years, that I should tell my story. I should write it down, put it in a book, and put it on tape. Tell about my life. I kept thinking, "Why? Who would want to hear about all these things in my life? Who would want to know all this mess? What good would this do for anyone?"

Three weeks after that conference was the "Women of Faith" conference in Lakeland, Florida. I thought, "Well!! OK God. I felt any opportunity God gave me during this time I needed to try to attend. I had money that needed to go for paying a bill and there was a charge for going to this conference. There were some women from our Church that were staying overnight. I felt like I was supposed to go. I thought, "How will I do this?" I took the money that was supposed to go toward this bill and paid it on my trip. It came down to the Friday morning of the day that we were going and I had some problems with the car (a new car that God had provided for me). I was going to drive to Lakeland that afternoon.

That morning, I went to attend our weekly prayer meeting. I was kind of mad with God that morning. I said: "God! I took my bill money, thinking that you wanted me to go to this and that you would provide the way for me. So far you haven't given me anything else and the bills are due. I am going to Lakeland. What is up with this! I am faithful. I have been following. I have been doing all the things you wanted me to do, and here I am."

We had a prayer meeting that morning and there were just a few of us there. They were asking how things were going. As we walked out

# LIFESONG - MY SYMPHONY

that day, one of the ladies handed me a fairly large amount of money. She said she just felt like it. God told her to give it to me. It not only was enough to re-pay me for what I had paid for the conference, but also was enough to pay for the due bill and buy a couple of books and things that I felt God wanted me to have when I was there at the "Women of Faith "conference. God really did come through, as only He does. If we are patient and wait long enough and trust him to do things in his time. Sometimes we really get into a desperate state before we realize what God is doing and what his timing is. We would do things differently, but God knows the best time to bless us and to share things with us. I headed on to Lakeland that afternoon with great expectations, once again feeling that God had something for me there.

I was not wrong! God had just wonderful things for me at that conference that day. It was so crowded! Thousands of women jam packed into this place. I vowed I would never go again unless they went to some larger place. (God heard me I guess. The next time they returned they went to an Arena in Orlando, a larger place.) During the first session each of them introduced themselves with tiny bits of information. Each one sounded very interesting, got my attention in so many different ways. As each speaker started to share their testimony and things from their lives, each one had portions that I would relate to.

There were some major issues that were brought home to me through the things that they had shared. I went back to the days of contemplating suicide. I was brought back to aspects of being attacked and violated in a physical manner. It just made me think of many things that had happened in my life. As I looked around me and I saw these women, I thought, "There are thousands of women sitting here, listening to these six ladies share their stories." Again God said, "I want you to write your story. I want you to put it on tape".

Again I asked, "Who would want to listen?" again God said, "Look around!" Then it hit home to me. "There are thousands of women here, listening to six ladies tell stories just like yours." I said: "OK God!" Friday night, Saturday - the sessions - each one was very good, each one had special things that were for me. I kept having these thoughts about my writing. It came time for lunch the last day. I was feeling very confused, all these old thoughts had returned to me, I just felt like I wanted to go off alone. I did. I went off alone. I picked up a quick bite to eat and I was thinking to myself that God was really impressing this on me, about telling my story. He also reminded me of things of the past and I pulled out my journal and started taking some notes about some of the things that God had reminded me of or brought back to me. Some of them I wasn't happy he reminded me of, this was supposed to be a joyful journey and I thought, "OK! Where is the joy?"

As the ladies had shared their testimonies, had brought out the fact of how God had brought them through and how joy was brought to them and restored in their lives, through some horrendous life circumstances. I was thinking, about all those things, wrote a little bit in my journal about that, and thinking that maybe I should just run away, not come back to the final session, leave it all there, and just leave. I just had this feeling that I should leave.

I wrote in my journal that God was telling me to write and tape my story. I indicated also in my writing that I was having thoughts again of suicide which I had not had for years. I did return to the conference for the final session and Lucy Swindall came to speak last. Her words were, "Life is tough, don't you love it?" just the way she said it, I knew I was going to like her. She went on and shared some very wonderful things out of her testimony, out of her life. The most important thing she had to say for me to hear was how God led her to write her first book.

That was like the nail driven home. I felt like "OK! I know what God is telling me. I've got to go home and do this" I had the feeling that God wanted me to do this while I was off from work, in this time of job seeking. As I returned home that day I re-listened to some of Joyce Meyer's tapes that I purchased a few weeks prior and all of it just re-iterated in me the fact that God wanted me to do this – write this book. Tell my story.

I continued on in my time of worship and study and intimacy with God. I was job seeking. I was going to interviews. I was putting in applications, but nothing seemed to work. I just kept following any lead I could get, any field I was involved with or qualified for and I just kept going and going (like the Eveready bunny) seeking out what employment might have been there for me. I began making some notes as far as what God wanted me to share out of my life, what to tell folks on tape or to write in a book. It all came very quickly as God gave me very specific things, things He wanted me to write about, tell. I went and talked to my pastor's wife and my pastor. Just as God was leading me to contact different people and tell them what I was doing, what God had led me to do; write them letters, make the phone calls and just work on it.

I was invited to speak, one Wednesday night, to a special ladies meeting we were having at church. I shared some of the high points from my notes for the book. I received a card in the mail, the following week from one of the ladies from Church that said, "I think you should write your story!" Again, it was another confirmation that God wanted me to do this thing. Then, I would be talking with people, making the contacts that God would lead me to do. The decision was made that I should do a tape first, a testimony tape so I would have at least something that I could share with folks until the book was finished. I thought I should sit and dictate the tapes of my story and then have them transcribed. There were some musical inserts I felt should be included since they were great influences on my life.

I began thinking about what God impressed on me. Sit at the keyboard and tell your story. I invited a few ladies from the prayer group and counseling group. I was going to go to the Church and sit at the keyboard and I got one of the fellows who did some of the taping at our Church. I was just going to sit there and tape it live, not a professional tape or anything like that, just sit there and share the things that God told me to share. I had prayer with some dear friends before I started. I began sharing my life from its beginning. God just gave me the things He wanted me to say.

I made a timeline of my life, my activities, and the music that was involved each period of my life. I found myself playing some of the music underneath as I was talking. People listening didn't realize it, or later as they listened to my tape, each thing that I was playing underneath my speaking had a specific meaning to me regarding what I was talking about at the time. We had an awesome time that night; only six or seven were there. There was one lady in particular, a leader in the counseling ministry, that came up afterworlds and we were talking and we just started crying together, because she realized that some of the things that I went through were some of the things she had dealt with in life. Even though she had dealt with those issues, it touched her to know that someone else had been through the same things, had shared the same sort of problems and same sort of hurts.

That re-iterated for me that, that's what it's all about; to reach people who had hurts, had problems, and let them know that someone else out there has been through the same things, and trusted God and made it. With God we can do all things.

I had a few people that God had placed on my heart to share the tape with. Some of those were a couple of people that I had met in the neighborhood bar. I took them a copy of the tape and began to share with them. God began to do wonderful, wonderful things, just by people listening to the tape. One lady and her husband started coming to me and asking me for prayer in regards to family issues. Some others came to me and dealt with problems that they had: abortion, other problems, and other things.

They shared how that was something that plagued them daily, as something that happened so much earlier in their lives. Others illicit sexual affairs, others addicted to alcohol and drugs, saying, "I don't want to be a drunk anymore!" God did such wonderful, miraculous things through just a few listening to the tape. A tape which was in no way professional, in no way done by a performer, just something to have to share.

God showed me very quickly that he had something mighty and powerful coming from these things. I continued on and made notes for the book and then I came into some job changes. God led me from my fast into a full time job (*The beginning of this book*). I wondered why God put me in the places he did in this job. He put me; first of all, in a place that was one of my favorite places on Disney property. He put me there in the middle of the night (which I asked for so I could continue things with the ministries). But I found myself out there, at night, looking up into the stars and skies just seeking God and praying for the people of Disney World as well as for the City of Orlando. The entire area: people involved with addictions, people involved with so many attacks from the devil. I would walk through those grounds at night and prayed over those things. Then God moved me from there to a lonely kiosk where it was only me and the mosquitoes; sometimes the birds were singing, sometimes a storm, rain falling, cold nights, various things. I thought, "OK! What am I doing out here in the middle of the night?" But God kept saying, "I want you to begin dictating your book". So, all the notes I had done, the preparation, I had started speaking in my kiosk.

Every night I would carry my recorder and tapes to work. Some nights I would start talking, recording. But other nights I would find myself unable to dictate. I had plenty of time to dictate the things on the book working grave shift. My particular Kiosk had about 2 hours each night that I had no or few vehicles enter. My manager knew that if I was talking (seemingly to myself) doing the taping it was keeping me awake and alert. I started and then I just drew cold. Each night I would have good intentions. But, each night, I just wouldn't get it done.

Finally, I got very concerned about it. (I am writing this right now, standing in the kiosk, listening to the rain, I just saw a little rabbit run across the road.) God impressed on me to get it done. This followed another period of fasting that God had led me into.

It was another one of those mornings that I thought God just wanted me to pray and praise him throughout the day. So, I began doing that. And then like the day when God said to me: "I want you to fast until…" and then I said, "Until what?" Then it was, "until I (God) give you a full time job", which He did immediately. So, what is this time for? I had been putting in for various job changes and promotions. God had placed on my heart to seek promotion. He tells us he will give us the desires of our heart and I truly felt that he put those particular jobs and interests on my heart. If I was going to be working

# LIFESONG - MY SYMPHONY

and had to be out there working to make a living, He would put those desires on my heart and make the way for me to do the jobs I would like to be doing. I had gone to several interviews, put in several applications, and a lot of them seemed good, seemed it was working, but nothing had happened yet. I kept wondering, "Why? What is going on here?" I just knew I needed to pursue promotion, wait for God's timing, and praise God always no matter what the outcome.

That day God wanted me to fast until…there is some sort of change. I assumed that meant a job change. I began fasting and praying and seeking God. God led me into a 15 day fast. Each day as I would get up it was easy for me to fast, it was probably the easiest time in my life as I was attempting to fast. It confirmed to me that it was definitely God directing me and guiding me to do this. Although I was studying all along, I began just re-reading continuously Psalms and Proverbs and several different translations, just reading them through over and over again. Finally, this one morning, I got up and I thought that somehow this is going to be the day; it's the 15th day. I was still fasting, still praying, and still carrying my tape recorder and tapes to work every night, still not doing any taping.

It was coming up time when Joyce Meyer was going to be here again, it had been a year since the first Women of Faith conference. I was able to go only to one session this time because of the way I was working. The Joyful Journey Ladies were returning with the conference Bring Back the Joy. Since the conference last year, I had written to Lucy Swindall twice and I shared with her God leading me to write my book. In the second letter I wrote that I had completed the testimony tape and I sent her a copy. I thought, "She is going to be in this conference, if I get an opportunity to speak to her that I need to share with her the progress of the book.

How will I tell her that I haven't done anything in the last four months?" So I was convicted, I better do something here. I knew that I was going with great expectations because of what happened the year prior at the conference. I went back to work that night and pulled out the tape recorder and began dictating. I didn't stop again. I continued until the dictation was finished. As I went to the conference, the Friday night session ended and I was going to work that night and then return from work to the conference on Saturday morning. They had a book signing section at the end of that evening and I had about an hour or more to kill before I had actually to leave and go to work. I hung around, looked at all the book tables and I felt there were several things God was impressing on me that would be good books and tapes to have for myself, as well as to share with other people. I looked at those, and then I went by the "Women of Faith" booth. I saw these things and I thought, sure would be neat to have this purple bag that I saw and I thought, "That would be neat but I don't need a tote bag".

I tried to rationalize with myself: its vinyl, would be very practical, it also has a zipper, which most of mine don't. I thought that even though God has blessed me with this job and some overtime, I am still trying to pay and catch up with bills and things. "No," God would want me to spend my money a little more wisely. If I buy anything I should buy some of the books and tapes that would be beneficial to my spiritual growth as well as someone else's. I passed on the tote and every time I would pass the booth I would think: "Wow! That's neat! Sure wish I could have that." I looked at a t-shirt and I thought: "I don't need another t-shirt".

They had a pin and I thought, "No! You don't need another pin either". I would go by there several times that Friday night and during the day Saturday thinking, "Would be nice to have some of these things! No! I cannot afford those. Even though God was blessing me financially, I could not afford to splurge on those unnecessary things".

I went by Lucy's table. I had been there several times and there were many people lined up to talk to her. I would go back later when the crowd was thinning out. She had one other person there, talking with her. I had decided to buy one of her books. I got the book and approached her to sign it when this other lady walked away. I began sharing with her about last year, my testimony, how she was the final confirmation to me that God would have me to write my book and tell my story, how I have written to her and things. We chatted a little bit about that and her final words were: "You know, that is what it's all about". I thought: "Yes! That is what it's all about. It's about doing what God had set in my mind and my heart that I should do. Maybe I can be an inspiration and help someone else to write his or her book. Tell their story. But, most of all have someone else realize that through Christ and through the spiritual walk, nothing in life is too hard. It might be tough but we can still love it because of the joy that God puts within us.

As I was walking Saturday through the conference hall I again passed the sales booth many times, looking at those tempting items. I noticed that they had a drawing box. You know! "Sign here for a prize". I thought, "I never win those things! Maybe I will win a gift certificate or something or maybe I would came back and get that bag". (Still thinking about that pretty purple bag that I wanted) I filled it out and put it in the box. I did this before the last session. During the night before as I was taping,

I was coming to parts in the tape that dealt with my days at Baptist Bible College and I thought, "I wonder if that would be really beneficial to that many people. Teaching Sign Language and all of that, Is there any reason to include all of that?" And wondering how much of that I should really include in the taping and writing. I was wondering about that as I went to the last session.

They had the drawing just prior to the last session. There were several ladies from my Church attending, scattered throughout the arena. The first name they pulled out from the box was Karen Twigg. This big cheer went up and I thought: "I won in the same Arena as Shaq O' Neill. Yes!" "Awesome!" After they read the six names that won the prizes, they held up one of the purple bags and they said, "If your name was called would you please stop by the booth outside to receive one of these bags with some goodies inside."

God is good. He is so faithful in the small things. Another thing that I thought about was: "Gee! I wish I had the message from last year, Lucy sharing about her writing her book, and the other things that the other ladies had shared. This year there were some things the same but also they had different approaches and different stories to share. I had my notes and things but I really wished I had a tape from last year.

After the session I was walking down to the booth to claim my prize and then I was going home to sleep quickly and then go back to work that night. I heard this voice calling my name. I turned around expecting to see one of the ladies from my Church group or someone that I knew from the City. I did not see anyone that I recognized (in the midst of faces: this year there were 50,000 women at the conference).

I paused for a moment and I heard a voice saying "Karen Twigg" I looked around again and I saw one lady looking at me. "Did you call my name?" and she said, "Yes!" she said, "Didn't they call your name a little while ago?" I said: "yes!" she said: "You went to Baptist Bible College - Right?" I said, "Yes I did!" she said, "You taught there?" I said: "Yes! Please forgive me I don't recognize you or remember your name". She said, "Oh! You wouldn't." She said, "I was never in your class, but I knew about you, knew about your teaching. This lady with me teaches sign and interprets for the deaf at my Church". That re-affirmed in me that the things I had done were important.

I did not know this lady, I still don't. I know that she lives somewhere on the coast of Florida. Because they called my name, she spotted me in the crowd, ten years after I was at Baptist Bible College teaching. She recognized and knew that I had done something apparently worthwhile at Baptist Bible College.

When I got to my car I opened the bag and looked inside. Inside was: a T-shirt saying "I am a Woman of Faith", one of the pins, a couple of tapes from last year's session and several other things. God just does so many wonderful things. The fact that He had them call my name was one thing and I got my bag. But the most important thing, the biggest thing that he had done was to reaffirm in me that things that I have done in my life have been worthwhile, had been beneficial, they had reached someone, somewhere. We never know who on the sidelines may be reached by something we have done or something we had said. (Good or bad.)

God gave me the reassurance that day, the reaffirmation that the things that I was doing were good, that they were right. I just knew in my heart that by telling my story and putting it on paper and on tapes were things that God wanted me to do and then somebody, somewhere was somehow going to benefit from it, as I did from the tapes and from the books and from the messages that I heard from these other women. Again, it was an awesome time in my life.

I was now working on the dictation again and had been so blessed by the conference. God said, "OK! It is finished" I said: "What's finished?" The fast was over because what God wanted was me to resume the taping. In 2 weeks the tapes were finished. God is so good, so faithful.

## Car Pit Crew

God very faithfully has helped me through the years with many, many car situations. I could write a book alone on things that happened with vehicles and cars and how God led and helped and supplied. Through vehicle problems I got to know very well 3 or 4 families in my Church that I did not know very well before. They would work on my car and I would get to know their wives and their families and I really appreciated the time that God gave me to know these families in my Church. Also they helped me get leads on cars for me to look at to buy.

One of the times I was sitting without a job, driving down the road in January. It was Super bowl Sunday, and I was driving to my brother's home. My car was making this strange noise; and then all of a sudden there was just a big sound as I pulled into his driveway. My engine had just, literally, come apart inside. We had this group of men at Church that had developed what they called a "Pit Crew". They would help, particularly, single ladies at the Church and once every three or four months they would get together and change the oil and kind of look over the vehicle and what have you.

So, I began calling some of these fellows. They were working with me in relation to my car. The car had 170,000 miles on it. After looking at it, they felt that it couldn't be repaired. As I was sitting there: I had no job again, no car again, just totally relying and trusting on God.

One of the families from the Pit Crew, within a day from when my car went out, came to me and said: "We have a vehicle you can use!" They indicated that there was one he was working on and repairing, getting ready to sell it. It wasn't one that his family needed, but was licensed. I could take it and drive it. God blessed miraculously because it was 3 to 4 months until I was able to replace mine. I had something to drive. They had lent me a vehicle. It was a bigger car than I was used to.

One night I was driving and I got a little carried away on the speed, because, as I said I wasn't used to the power of the vehicle. I was in an area where I knew police stopped people all the time. I knew to be careful. I got stopped and got a ticket. Not only that, I almost got carried to jail because there had been a problem with the license plate. What had happened was their neighborhood kids had switched license plates as a prank and they weren't aware that this had been done. It looked like I was driving a car with a stolen tag and I just barely avoided going to jail. But, God works so many wonderful things.

The Pit Crew pulled together and they started searching for a vehicle. They knew I didn't have much money; my brother was going to help me some. That I had to spend just a couple of hundred dollars, that I had to try to get something that was decent and drivable enough so that I could at least maintain my part time job and also maintain the job search. Therefore it would have to bring me to the interviews and to the things at Church.

In April, God led us to a car that was super reasonable, that was in good shape, and the fellows checked it out. They thought it was a great buy. They had also gathered some money towards the purchase of my vehicle. With their help and the help of my brother we were able to purchase that car and I was on the road again.

## *Pageants*

One of the ladies that I met on my job at Disney was a lady that worked with pageants. Through working together, we learned of our backgrounds involving pageants. We talked pageants. She was a director of the Miss Orlando Pageant, a Miss America preliminary. After talking with her and sharing our pageant stories she invited me to come and help. The first year I assisted them as their talent coordinator working with the girls and their talents. They began to see more of what I could do and what my background was. The next year they asked me to totally produce and direct the show itself. Then I began doing that and I started bringing in a crew from my Church. That included: sound people, light people, all the technical people, someone to do some of the singing and a co-MC, people to assist me in the directing. People were impressed with the staff that I brought in.

How we worked together and how they didn't have to worry about us following the rules and their directions and things that they set down for us. It was a very good crew to work with. We impacted the city because of our work together and our productions. We grew to where we had 30 some people assisting us with the Miss Orland pageant production each year from church. We had many opportunities to witness and share. We had families come to our Church as a result of our outreach at Miss Orlando. There were others we had personal opportunities to witness to.

I believe God led me into pageants also as a ministry. We worked well together and each one, each year kept getting better. It was a very awesome opportunity that we had. As I continued my involvement with pageants, Leslie had gone on to other things.

My life then consisted of: my Church, where I did counseling, where I ministered with the women's groups, where I was involved with the worship team and playing the keyboards and doing the music secretarial work. I loved praise and worship. I had various opportunities as I ministered not only with people involved with drugs and alcohol, but with friendships that I formed through the pageants, people that I was trying to help. I assisted some in court with their legal battles, but most of all with their spiritual battles. My heart's desire is for them to recognize that the only true answer for them in life, the only true high, the only true buzz comes from their relationship with God and the Lord Jesus Christ.

## *The Grill Room*

I had a ministry in a little neighborhood bar where I talked to people and shared with a lot of people who will never set foot in a Church. I did it as I think Jesus would do it. I go to where they are and invite them to come out.

**A side note – I do like to enjoy life and have fun. Riding the motorcycle is a great thrill. Skydiving is awesome – reminds me of soaring with the eagles.**

*Isaiah 40:31*
*But they that wait upon the Lord shall renew their strength; they shall mount up with wings like the eagles; they shall run, and not be weary; and they shall walk, and not faint.*

I loved to go to Church, loved to pray and worship, loved to hear the gospel as it is preached, and I continued learning and growing. I spent a lot of my own personal time away from anything else, listening to praise and worship music and inspirational tapes or challenging tapes by a variety of people. I shared in ministry. These are the things that I was involved with as well as my job. I had many opportunities to share. God showed me that he had put me in particular jobs, on particular shifts, to reach particular people. I never questioned why God put me somewhere, I just went and I did it.

I don't know what the future holds, but I do know who holds the future. I pray that as you read this, somewhere through these pages you will receive a blessing, you will receive an answer, you will receive a call, you will receive the love of the Lord Jesus Christ and you will know that God is reaching out his hand to you and asking you to take his hand. Let him lead you on and show you the way.

*1 Thessalonians 5:24*
*Faithful is he that calleth you, who also will do it.*

## LIFESONG - MY SYMPHONY

# CHAPTER 8:
# THE ENCORE – LAST FEW YEARS

It has taken several years to get from tapes to print. There have been 4 different people agree to transcribe the tapes. Each one took tapes, would begin and then things kept interfering with their continuing. Each one was someone God would connect to me; have me meet on life's journeys. Finally – Thanks Anna Marie – they were complete. Then I began the task of editing and correcting my errors. I did not have a lot of spare time so I would grab moments here and there. That took me a couple years, especially on vacations and off times. God led me to take a week vacation and fast until I finished. I had 9 days off. It took me 8 days of constant work with a few family activities, church activities and volunteer activities intertwined. Then more proofreading – Thanks Carol, Missy, CG, Liz and other careful readers - and it is finished, ready to print.

It was several years (more than I expected) before this book ever came to print. In God's time, It is finished.

Since the days in the Kiosk I moved up the ranks at Disney. There have been many applications and interviews. There have been rejections and promotions. Sometimes I had to really pursue but I remained persistent. I continued praising God each step of the way – through the promotions and the rejections. I progressed from Shopper to Security Hostess, to Resort security Officer (they did away with that job – too bad because I really loved that job), back to Security Hostess, to Loss Prevention Specialist, to Security Manager. I was devastated when they took away the Resort Security Officer Job. But I realize had they not done so I would not have progressed to where I did. Sometimes we get too comfortable where we are to realize God wants us to move on to promotion and greater blessing. Other times, He wants us to wait and see how we handle the rejection. Do we praise Him anyway?

From the kiosk I met some co-workers that were interested in studying more of the Bible so I started a Bible Study with 2 of them. Through several years together God greatly enriched our lives through our study. Other people joined us and I called us an Encouragement Team.

That is what we did. We met, shared God's word, various tapes and sermons, brought prayer requests and praise reports, but, most of all, we supported and encouraged one another through life.

I stopped working with the pageants because they took so much time. I wanted to devote more time to the writing of this book and other ministry. God opened a new volunteer window for me. My focus, as that of many others, has changed since September 11th. I became a Board Member of a Community Emergency Response Team (CERT) in Seminole, County Florida and involved with Critical Incident Stress Management (CISM). The past several years have been filled with much training and many classes related to these activities as well as meetings and drills. It is another way God has me serving people. In 2007 I became a board member of the Florida State Emergency Response Team and completed hours for CISM certification.

God led me to attend Faithworld Church under the ministry of Pastor Clint Brown. (*He was the one I heard sing at that first Joyce Meyer Conference.*) My mother kept asking me, "Aren't you playing at all?" It is the first church in my life that I have not been playing in some capacity the piano, organ, or keyboards. I knew God wanted me to just go there to praise and worship him.

After a few months in the congregation I believed God wanted me to join the choir as a praiser and worshiper. I have been there ever since. In talking with one of the pastors when I first went to Faithworld, he learned of my work with the deaf and Sign Language. He told me that he and his wife had been praying for a deaf ministry at Faithworld. That pricked my heart, I prayed about it, and God directed me back to that pastor and I told him I believed I should start that ministry.

## *Deaf Ministry - A New Beginning*

We changed the name from deaf ministry to Visual Language Ministry because signing is not just for the deaf anymore. There are autistic, stroke victims, cerebral palsied and others that now communicate using Sign Language. There are others who do not know the language but receive added blessing to their praise by just watching the Visual Language.

We have been training interpreters for a few years now and have raised up some awesome sign praisers. There have been struggles in the growing ministry and even attacks from within but God has shown us that this is His ministry and nothing can destroy it if we remain faithful through the struggles and the good times. We are preparing interpreters to become certified with the Registry of Interpreters for the Deaf so we can have an even greater impact on our community.

This is an example of how God moves us from ministries or outreaches at times in our life, we may think those seasons are over, but we do not know when he may resurrect those things again. I thought my days working with the deaf and Sign Language were over. But we built an awesome ministry. It is another group that supports one another, encourages one another and prays for one another and the Deaf of the community. Most importantly, we praise and worship together through sign which takes us deeper into God's presence.

## *Issue Of Blood*

As I started Faithworld I was entering yet another time of illness. I was going through the change of life (I had prayed for that for years) and was having an issue with blood. So many times through that year I would make myself go to work and church feeling like I had no energy and was not sure if I would have the energy to stand, let alone sing or sign.

Our choir would sing and move, takes a lot of energy. Many times I did not have the energy for both. I would sort of move and mouth the words. But I knew that if I would just continue to praise my way through that God would touch me. So many times through those months, pastor or guest speakers would talk about the woman with the issue of blood. Every time I would praise and claim healing for myself. One time pastor was preaching and talking about how we have the same power within us yet we think we have to go to the Lord through someone else to be healed. He said we should be able to lay hands on ourselves, pray for ourselves in the same way it was done for others. I did that and continued to praise God. God began to heal me. I could feel healing within my body.

# LIFESONG - MY SYMPHONY

I did not go to the doctor because I needed to make some insurance changes. After several months I was able to make those insurance changes and I went to the doctor. He immediately became concerned because my blood counts were so low. He told me that if they had dropped that low quickly I would be dead. I told him that I had already been getting better than I had been. I told him that I believed that God had already taken care of whatever it was and my body was healing. He believed God could heal but he also wanted me to have some tests. The specialist doing the test looked at my counts and said that must be wrong, they can't be that low.

He called my doctor to verify that he had received the correct information. He told me I must have cancer somewhere in my body. *(The devil is a liar)* I told him I believed that whatever had been there was healed and that I am getting better. He ran every test imaginable and could find nothing wrong. My counts kept coming up but they were not treating me for anything. I thank God for the healing that he brought to me through my praise and belief standing in the choir and signing. *(For a while I had to sit to sign because I did not have the energy to stand.)*

I was involved with a Morning Prayer group until my schedule did not allow it. I go to the church whenever they need volunteers. I do some counseling. I attend every service on Sundays (2 or 3 every week) even after I had worked all night. I attend Tuesday evening services and Monday evening Sign Language classes and choir/worship team rehearsals. I attended Thursday morning services (when they had them) occasionally as my schedule allowed. I believe that God's message for me comes from there and I don't want to miss anything he wants to tell me nor do I want to miss an opportunity to praise and worship him.

My brother became homebound from work a few years ago so I began preparing his major meals and taking care of his laundry. My mother would come a couple times a year and spend a month or so which would give me a break until she made her journey to heaven a few years ago. Then we got someone to come in and clean his house but I was still doing all the cooking and laundry. My sister moved to Florida so then we shared some of those responsibilities.

My Pastor Clint Brown has taught me many things. Because of his teachings and the conviction I had for so long, I am now in better standing with the credit bureau. My sister and I purchased a home together, first in our lives. It was a fantastic blessing. My favorite room was my music room, quiet room. God touched someone's heart and they blessed me with a piano. I had not had one at home for years. I studied and praised in that room.

In the last season before publishing this book we fell into some financial difficulties so my sister and I sold our house. She is with my brother as he has had a very rough few years of injuries and rehab – 1 ½ years in hospitals and rehab. I still help with cooking and care for him.

I am in an apartment made just for me. I still have my 'Blue Room' with my piano and place for study. I also have a magnificent screened patio with a great nature view – trees, shrubs, squirrels, lizards, and a ravine. My rocking chair and plants provide a great place for relaxation, reading, and study. That's where I am sitting writing these last paragraphs of LifeSong.

Leslie has returned to Florida – called of God to be here. We work together there in the sign ministry and other church functions as well as jail ministry. God knew this mother's heart was lonely and he brought Leslie back. It is so awesome to see her heart of praise and worship, her love for God, and her outreach to so many.

My granddaughter is now a beautiful young woman who also has a love of God. She is working and college bound.

God has promoted me to now be the leader of all the volunteers at Faithworld. As a result of my serving God He has called me to be a leader of His servants. We have also started a Minister In Training (MIT) program at Faithworld and Pastor Brown has asked me to oversee their training. The teacher in me is still at work.

I have retired from Disney so now I have time for more service in ministry and finally LifeSong Ministry.

I thank God for all he has brought me through and the blessings He has poured out. I praise Him for the blessings from this book.

### *23 Psalm*

*The Lord is my shepherd; I shall not want. He maketh me to lie down in green pastures; he leadeth me beside the still waters. He restoreth my soul, he leadeth me in the path of righteousness for his name's sake. Yea, though I walk through the valley of the shadow of death, I will fear no evil; for thou art with me; thy rod and thy staff they comfort me. Thou preparest a table before me in the presence of mine enemies; thou anointest my head with oil; my cup runneth over. Surely goodness and mercy shall follow me all the days of my life; and I will dwell in the house of the Lord forever.*

# CHAPTER 9: FINALE – NOT YET

The *LifeSong* finale has not yet been written. I know it will be grand and I know God is not finished with me yet. He has given me many dreams and vision of things to come. Some I have been expecting since my youth and some newer insights. I know God will bring those to pass. I do not wonder when or how? I just ask Him for daily guidance and his accompaniment each step of the way. The end of this book is not the end of my *LifeSong*. The Finale is yet to come. I pray God will bless millions as they read this book or hear me share my *LifeSong* in person. He told me they will.

I will continue my life following God's direction and relying on my life's verse.

*Joshua 1:9*
*Have not I commanded thee? Be strong and of good courage; be not afraid, neither be thou dismayed; for the Lord your God is with thee wherever thou goest.*

# LIFESONG - MY SYMPHONY

www.ingramcontent.com/pod-product-compliance
Lightning Source LLC
LaVergne TN
LVHW041627070426
835507LV00008B/485